Rocky Roads

The Journeys of Families through Suicide Grief

Michelle Linn-Gust, Ph.D.

Rocky Roads: The Journeys of Families through Suicide Grief
Copyright © 2010 by Michelle Linn-Gust.

All rights reserved. No portion of this book may be reproduced—mechanically, electronically, or by any other means, including photocopying—without written permission of the publisher.

ISBN: 978-09723318-1-4

Library of Congress Control Number: 2010903019

Chellehead Works books are available at special discounts when purchased in bulk for premiums and sales promotions as well as fundraising and educational use.

For details, contact the Special Sales Director at:

info@chelleheadworks.com

505-266-3134 (voice)

Albuquerque, New Mexico

Printed in the United States of America

First printing March 2010

Designed by Megan Herndon

Cover photo:

Taken in My Son, Vietnam, home of the lost civilization Champa, by my husband, Joe Gust, in October 2004. When I told him that I was going to name the book *Rocky Roads*, he said, "I have just the photo for you," and he found it in his files. The rocky road is a reminder that while grief is taxing and difficult, it is a challenge that we can survive. We can look back on the road and say, "Wow, look how far I've come and what I've achieved."

> *"The book is lovely. I know that probably sounds like a strange word, and it's not one I use very often, but somehow it's the one that rises for me. Something about how straight-forward and sensitive Michelle's writing is, never being the "expert" above it all, and raising questions without having to always have an answer. I think it fills a need and hope for the best with its success."*
>
> *- Donna L. Schuurman, EdD, FT*
>
> *Executive Director, The Dougy Center for Grieving Children & Families*

CONTENTS

Acknowledgments 1

Introduction 3

The Road Map 7

Suicide
1. The Language of Suicide and Grief 9

2. Suicide: How Did I End Up on This Grief Journey? 13

3. The Suicide Grief Experience 21

The Family
4. Introduction: Families and Suicide 43

5. What is a Family? 44

6. The Family as a System 45

7. Relationship Losses in the Family 50

8. Other Family Relationships and Grief 58

9. The Lifespan and Grief 64

10. The Family Unit's Grief Reaction 71

Finding Hope
11. Directions 81

12. Checking the Map 100

13. Notes for Caregivers, Clinicians, Friends,
    and Other Supports 107

Afterword 113

References 117

Resources 121

In Memory of my German Shepherd dog Daisy "LuLu," whose terminal cancer diagnosis and subsequent death helped me to finish *Rocky Roads* when I needed something to focus my energy and find hope.

"Hope is to the spirit what oxygen is to the lungs. It fuels energy and efforts to rise above adversity."
– *Froma Walsh (Walsh, 2003)*

- Acknowledgments -

Many, many people helped this project come to fruition over the past five years. A big thanks to everyone around the world who supported me and waited patiently for me to finish this book among the other million things I'm working on. Thank you to JoAnn Sartorius who helped me shape and mold my initial idea for *Rocky Roads* (and the title) on many trips throughout New Mexico en route to presenting workshops on suicide. Thank you to Julie Cerel, Myfawny Maple, Peter Wolheim, and my mom, Marianne Linn, for the draft comments. And thank you to the people whom without this project wouldn't have been possible: editor Beth Hadas, designer Megan Herndon, and web guy Tim Mickey. And finally to my husband Joe for understanding that the writer in me has to do her thing. A pat on the head to Chaco, Nestle, Hattie, and our newest addition, Gidget, for reminding me that there is life beyond my laptop.

- Introduction -

In the seventeen years since my sister died, I've had my own grief experience. I've had the grief experience of my family. And I've learned a lot from the people I've interacted with throughout the world. In the almost nine years since my first book, *Do They Have Bad Days in Heaven? Surviving the Suicide Loss of a Sibling,* was published, I've watched siblings come out and seek help from each other—and teach their parents that they need help and support. While parallels have run through the stories, none are exactly alike.

In that time, we have learned to do a better job discussing how the individual relationships within families are impacted by grief. But we have still left out the family unit. It was during my doctoral work in family studies that I came to realize the importance of the family as a system and how we've neglected it. I often think of LaRita Archibald's story as the best example of how a family is changed after the suicide of one member. After LaRita's son Kent (one of her five children) killed himself, she struggled to learn how to cut a pie for the family without Kent. For so many years, she had cut it for seven people. Without Kent, there were only six Archibalds left to eat the pie. Even though Kent is not part of the Archibald family in a physical sense, he always will affect the choices they make. And the bond isn't broken. He always will be part of the family. The Archibalds are no different from any other family with a suicide loss. The loved one retains family membership.

I have watched my own family grieve and somehow stay together, even with that empty chair at the dining-room table at holidays. In time, we filled the chair with other people and relationships. We talked about Denise together, but we also grieved separately. This book came about because, while watching my family and other families grieve, I began to wonder, Why is it that some families can work through their suicide loss and be stronger than before while others get stuck and cannot come back together as a family unit?

Introduction

The family is the most significant social group in which grief is experienced yet we have written little about the family unit after a suicide.

My goal in writing this book is to guide the family unit through suicide grief. I have tried to provide at least a little bit of every piece of family grief possible. In places where I know there are more comprehensive sources, I offer them for people who want to learn more about a particular area or topic. This book is not a story about my family: I told that story in my first book. Instead, it is a compilation of what people have taught me along my grief journey, mostly since the release of that first book in 2001. I do include aspects of my own grief journey, and I will explain why in the next chapter, "The Road Map."

I am not a therapist or a counselor. People tell me their stories because I am visible. I have done countless presentations to educate people on suicide and the losses it leaves behind. My goals are to make people aware of how to help someone who might be suicidal, to let them know they can survive suicide if they are faced with a loss in their lives, and to teach them how to help other people they know who are grieving a suicide loss.

While research on suicide grief has expanded significantly in the past several years, it is still limited by hesitancy on the part of the people who govern the research process to ask those bereaved by suicide to take part in studies. The bulk of the existing research is limited in several ways: not following the bereaved for long enough periods of time to see meaningful change, lack of theory-based research, lack of uniform research protocols. I have included as many references as possible, but some information is anecdotal, from stories people have told me. The expansion of research that we hope for will offer more opportunities for treatment and and more interventions for people coping with suicide loss.

The concept of postvention, helping people after the suicide, is important on many levels. At the individual level, the most basic of all, we want to assist people on this grief journey because it is a confusing time in a person's life. We want to let people know that they will be okay, that they will laugh again. And they will see hope again. On a larger scale, suicide affects entire communities when it happens. These communities include schools, workplaces, churches, activities, neighborhoods, and any other place people find a sense of belonging. Between the individual and the community is the family, the reason I wrote *Rocky Roads*. The purpose of this book is to help the family process what has happened, both by assisting individual family members with personal grief and, on a larger scale, to help the family unit. Without postvention after the devastating loss of suicide, people risk losing hope for the future. Postvention is prevention for the next generation.

Because *Do They Have Bad Days in Heaven?* was published eight years after Denise died, I had ample time to trudge along my road. I started work on it in 1996, when I was a high school health teacher, and I remember how frustrating it was when people would come to me and tell me how much they needed the resource. Not until 2000 did I find a publisher. I understood that it had taken that long because I still had some lessons to learn so that I could educate other people. The book wouldn't have been what it was supposed to be if it had been published any earlier. And since then, I have been honored that people around the world have shared their stories, their struggles, the loved ones they have lost, with me. It is because of all these people bereaved by suicide worldwide that I have been able to write this book.

I hope that your grief journey does not feel insurmountable. While the road might be rocky, it is trekkable. And we can look back and see how far we've come, grateful to have made it this far, realizing that we were stronger than we thought. I know because I have been there.

THE ROAD MAP

"Follow me and I'll walk you past the pain"
- *Mickey Coleman from the song*
"Miss You More than Words Can Say"

Sometimes all we need is a road map, a guide to help us see what might be ahead. Grief, particularly suicide grief, may be unknown to most of us, and our individual journeys, including those within the family unit, will not be the same, yet the goal is for everyone to end up in the same place, somewhere on the road.

Grief will be unique for each of us. The rocky road of grieving is terrain that is unfamiliar to most of us. We might think we know how we would react after the loss of a loved one, but that isn't always how it works out. There is no direct path through grief, and we won't all travel quite the same road. It's not easy—in fact it may well be the most challenging passage in our lives. And just as each person's grief journey will be unique, so will the journeys of families. What one family might experience, another family might not encounter. Yet there are similarities in these paths that we will choose as we venture through grief. My hope is that you take what you need from this book and leave the rest. We have unique needs in grief. Everything won't be applicable to your family, but something you learn here might be later as the journey changes.

I tend not to think of the grief experience as all bad. I accepted a long time ago that I couldn't bring my sister back and instead believe, as Lois Bloom once said about her son's death, "Sam and I had more choices after Sammy died because Sammy made his choice to end his life." We have choices about where we go from this point and what we do with our lives.

Although this book is not about my personal grief journey, my years of speaking publicly have shown me that aspects of my own story can help people with their own grief journeys much as I have learned from reading autobiographies. I will share where I feel it will be helpful to others. During the seventeen years that have gone by since Denise died, I've lived quite a bit of life and learned a lot.

Some facets of suicide grief are not yet based in scientific research. While I don't believe that scientific research is the end all, it is key to the funding of new programs and the creation of new interventions that are important to helping people cope. Research honors the importance of suicide, and it is important in helping us better understand what kinds of programs work for what groups and individuals. The suicidology field as a whole is young (started only in the late 1940s) and the study of suicide bereavement wasn't included until the 1960s. This book is a combination of experience and research. As much as possible, I have cited research when it was available, giving readers a chance to seek out more information on a topic.

However, I also believe that personal experiences are important, and I've tried to balance the two as much as possible. One's focus in the grief experience should be on examining what he or she is coping with, on the family experience, and on how to make it stronger instead of relying simply on what others say via research. What others say is important in that it helps us to feel connected. It also validates our own experience. But it is not the most important piece of helping us cope. Reaching deep inside ourselves and focusing on our individual experience is.

When I was developing the concept of *Rocky Roads*, my New Mexico workshop co-presenter JoAnn Sartorius said, "*Rocky Roads* sounds more like an adventure. And something that is doable." That's exactly it. None of us chose this journey. Instead, we choose how we react to it and what we can make of our lives, and the lives of our families, from this point forward.

Rocky Roads is here to serve as a guide. As the grief journey rolls out in front of you, you choose how to maneuver it and *Rocky Roads* will be your road map. As you travel the road, you will see yourself change and your feelings evolve when you get to a new place. What might anger you at one point will not bother you at all later on. Do not be afraid of what is ahead and of what you do not know. That is part of the journey, and you will be surprised when you look back at how far you've come.

SUICIDE

1. The Language of Suicide and Grief

The language of suicide is partially responsible for the stigma and shame associated with it. While we were all taught "sticks and stones may break my bones, but names will never hurt me," I do not believe that to be true. Labels, as we call them now, often are painful and make coping difficult. It is hard enough to wrestle with grief without having to deal with the language around it too. Still, it is important for us to take time to examine some of the words we use surrounding suicide and grief and then explain how they will be used in this book.

Not so long ago the term *suicide survivors* was the only accepted phrase in the United States for people coping with suicide loss. As I mentioned in my first book for sibling suicide survivors, it was a phrase I never was comfortable using. Edwin Shneidman, the founder of studying suicide, coined the term *suicide survivors* in the 1960s. He used it to define anyone directly affected by a suicide, which usually included the immediate family (we will revisit that later). As the movement gained momentum, this was the term used. It can be confusing, though, because attempters often consider themselves survivors of suicide.

When I began to work internationally, I discovered that in other parts of the world the term is *bereaved by suicide,* which I believe is a more appropriate way to describe someone coping with suicide loss. Ultimately, both attempters and people who are grieving a suicide death are survivors of suicide, but I believe that each group deserves its own name, and I'm inclined to believe the term *survivors* better describes attempters. While we all seek to find hope again in our lives, we also need to feel we belong somewhere before we can move forward together.

The only possible issue I have heard with the term *bereaved by suicide* is that bereavement can have an expiration date. After people have been bereaved by suicide for many years, they may stop feeling so bereaved. Perhaps they have moved to a new place along the road. I have debated this since my sister died seventeen years ago, and think that if someone asked what I am, I would now say, "I am Michelle."

The process of writing this book enabled me to understand why I wasn't happy with the word *survivor*. I had thrown the question out to a group of colleagues: researchers, survivors, and some who are both, to ask them what they thought: *survivor of suicide* or *bereaved by suicide*? They came back to me with an array of answers that also included other phrases like *survivor after suicide* or *suicide-bereaved*. What I realized then was that who I am dictated what name I was most comfortable using.

In high school, I didn't have one group of friends with whom I spent all my time. I had friends from various groups and I liked it that way. I enjoyed the variety, and I thought I had lots of friends. I never saw myself defined by the friends I had or the activities I participated in at school. And when the word *survivor* was thrown at me, I didn't like that either. I'm just not comfortable using a single word or phrase. I prefer to state that my sister Denise died by suicide in 1993. It is simple and to the point.

But if I have to pick one term over the other, I will say I am bereaved even though where I am with her death is not where I was five, ten, or fifteen years ago. I also might say that I am a "survivor of suicide loss" as another option. This road is still evolving in front of me. *Bereaved by suicide* and *survivors of suicide loss* are terms I will use throughout this book, though I also use the word *survivor* from time to time.

The study of suicide, known as suicidology, originated in the 1940s with Shneidman and three Los Angeles colleagues: Norman Farberow, Robert Litman, and Mickey Heilig. The work that these four men began is what almost every piece of the three pillars of the field are built on: prevention, intervention, and postvention. Prevention is everything that comes before even thoughts of suicide (also known as suicide ideation). This includes education, to teach people the warning signs to look for and what resources are available if they are worried about someone they care about.

Intervention is what Living Works Education (a suicide prevention training organization based in Canada) calls "suicide first aid or "suicide CPR." It is identifying someone who is thinking about suicide or who might have a plan to attempt suicide and getting them help. Postvention is what comes after the attempt or the loss—it is helping the people who are left behind find hope again. And as Shneidman said, postvention after suicide is prevention for the next generation (Shneidman, 1972)). By helping the bereaved through their losses, we support their efforts to find life-sustaining hope again. By providing this support we are breaking the legacy of suicide in families.

Often, when discussing suicide, people will say that someone "committed suicide." Some cultures and religious denominations view suicide as something that goes against the natural order of life. People are not supposed take their own lives by because it runs counter to what we are taught to believe, that life is something to be cherished. In many places, suicide was considered a crime until as recently as fifty years ago.

Criminalization or condemnation of suicide can be a deterrent. For some suicidal people the fear of committing a crime by ending one's life or the idea of going to a not-so-desirable afterlife is enough to discourage a lethal attempt at suicide. But for the bereaved, for the people left behind after the loss, the condemnation of suicide can stigmatize the event and make them feel afraid or embarrassed to seek help or admit how a loved one died. Depending on their values and beliefs, it can mean a loved one committed a crime or a sin.

There are other ways to convey that someone ended a life by suicide. For instance, I use *died by suicide*. It is simple and to the point. Some people use it as a verb: *she suicided*. Others will say that someone "completed suicide" although that raises the question of the number of times they attempted before they made a lethal attempt.

A word I choose never to use regarding either the person who died or the person who is bereaved: *victim*. The word *victim* takes away our strength. Even when we are discussing someone who died by suicide, I do not believe this was a weak person. He or she was coping with something that many of us will never quite understand. As for the bereaved, I believe people who are coping with a loss are strong people, traveling a road that not everyone will understand. *Victim* strips that away. People coping with suicide loss are survivors of a suicide loss, and everyone should use words that emit that strength.

Other words that I choose not to use are *closure* and *moving on*. I do not believe that *closure* is a correct term for what we experience in suicide grief. That word makes it sound as if we close the book on a life that has ended and we place it in the bookcase, never to be opened again. That person remains with us for the rest of our lives, although in a different form. He or she still affects who we are. And the same with moving on. Yes, we move forward without them, but they are still with us because they helped form who we are, as their deaths affect who we become with the new choices in front of us.

Often we believe we know what grief is because of what we have viewed on television or in the movies. We could call this the propaganda of grief. Sometimes we see a parent who does not share his or her grief with a child, or we run into a person who chooses a self-destructive route through life, using the suicide as the excuse for those poor decisions. Experiences like this can hinder our own grief processes. It is important that we spend time to educate ourselves on grief and how we can work through it.

According to Webster's Dictionary, grief is mental suffering or distress over loss; sharp sorrow; painful regret (1996). Through dissecting this definition we can learn volumes about grief. For instance, it might not always be about the death loss of a person in our lives. Sometimes we grieve the loss of an opportunity or a friend who has left our lives. But as we are using the word for the purpose of this book, it is sharp sorrow—the pain of someone dying can feel like the stabbing pain of something hurting us. And it can be full of painful regret that we were not there for the person and/or that we did not tell them how much we cared about them. *Grief* is the noun but *grieving* is the verb—the feeling and the journey we have embarked on after our loved ones have died.

Webster's defines *bereave* as to deprive, especially by death (1996). An example would be that we are "bereaved after suicide loss." *Mourning* is defined as the expression of sorrow (or grief) that one feels after someone has died. While these are the most basic words to describe the loss, they do not give the full picture of the loss we experience after a suicide.

One issue with the language of suicide is how often people believe they have to explain what they are saying. Some people are uncomfortable with describing what *survivor of suicide* or *suicidology* means. I have always looked at it as an opportunity to educate people about something of which everyone should be aware. The number of suicides in the world far eclipses the number of deaths attributed to many other causes. Everyone should have some understanding of suicide, and it is only through teaching people that we can make that possible.

Just as each person's and each family's road map is unique, so also will they all find the appropriate language to describe what they experience individually. Some people will read the previous paragraphs and know exactly where they fit. Others will feel they are settling for something with which they do not completely agree. And yet others will search out other words, or choose none at all, to describe their emotions.

2. Suicide: How Did I End Up on This Grief Journey?

When a loved one dies by suicide, the bereaved are left with a stack of questions and a life that ceases to exist as the surviving loved one once knew it. There will be no more new experiences or growth with that person. The bereaved wonder: How did we get here? Why did my loved one kill him or herself? How could this happen to my family?

Before we discuss suicide and the hows and whys of its happening, it is important to understand why suicide elicits such strong emotions in the bereaved. Some people react in anger while it causes others to retreat.

Even more basic than suicide, how do we react to death? Our society has removed death from the home although we have made a turn back toward allowing people to die at home surrounded by family. For some people, though, it remains something that happens far away, in a hospital. Death is often a theme in fictional accounts (including films like *Ordinary People* or books like *The Lovely Bones*) or in biographies where people succeed in ways they weren't expected to, having forged ahead because of a loss that altered their lives. Is it because we often are not allowed to express our emotions that they can have such dramatic constructive or destructive effects on our lives?

Whatever the case, our view of suicide is based in our view of death. Do we remember our first experience with death? Was it traumatic (maybe even a suicide?) or was it the natural passing of a beloved grandparent after a long life? How did our family members react? Were we allowed to attend the funeral? Or have we had any experience with death before the suicide that brings us to read this book?

Once we understand our experience with death, then we need to take some time to process our experience with suicide. Have we lost a loved one to suicide prior to this current loss? Did we attempt suicide in our own lives? Or are we simply reacting to the cultural and religious beliefs that have been handed to us in our personal development? Before my sister died by suicide, I had known several people who attempted suicide but, to me, suicide was something that happened to other people—or to people on television. Even when I saw or read portrayals of families as very normal and loving and still having suicide, it never occurred to me that it could happen in my own.

Therapists, counselors, social workers, and all the other people who work with suicidal clients and the families left behind see that their own experiences with death and suicide affect how they react to the bereaved and the experience of a suicide loss. What are those experiences? Their fear of their own past (maybe their own suicide attempt?) Their own suicide loss they never were allowed to process? Their religious or cultural beliefs? These experiences affect how they treat people who hover too close to the suicide line.

People working through a loss find it hard to comprehend why therapists sometimes pull away when, as helping professionals, they should be there. Often even professionals have not been educated on suicide. Even if they are interested in learning more, the resources they need might not be available where they are. Fortunately, this situation is improving, although more work remains.

Suicide by Numbers

In the United States, approximately 33,000 people each year die by suicide. In 2006, the most recent year of data available as of the publishing of this book, 33,300 people in the United States died by suicide (McIntosh, 2009). About every fifteen minutes, a person in the United States ends his or her life. The World Health Organization (2010) estimates that almost a million people die by suicide each year. This translates to a suicide every forty seconds somewhere in the world.

We often say that these figures are estimated because we do not actually know how many people die by suicide. Some suicides are classified as accidents. People may fear that insurance companies will not pay life insurance claims when a death is ruled a suicide, although this belief is not necessarily correct. In addition, because of the stigma that surrounds suicide, it appears that when possible, a suicide will be classified as something else to protect the loved ones.

Of those 33,300 suicides in the United States, 26,308 are males. In general men use more lethal means (such as guns; roughly half those suicides were by firearm) while women have a tendency to use pills (perhaps more as a plea for help) although their firearm use is increasing. Ethnically, 30,138 of these people were white. Of the total number of suicides, middle-aged men (45 to 64) lead the numbers with 9,039 suicides. While the national rate of suicides per 100,000 white men is 19.8, the next leading group is Native Americans (both male and female) at 12.3.

The five states with the highest rate of suicide in 2006 were (in this order), Wyoming, Alaska, Montana, Nevada, and New Mexico. Wyoming's number of suicides per 100,000 people was 22.5. The national average in the United States is 11.1 per 100,000. If the U.S. as a whole were a state, it would be No. 37 on the list.

Overall, suicide is the eleventh leading cause of death for all age groups (heart disease and cancer are Nos. 1 and 2, respectively) (McIntosh, 2009). For the fifteen-to-twenty-four age group, however, it is the third leading cause behind accidents and homicide.

The United States does not keep solid national data on suicide attempts. McIntosh (2009) estimates that 832,500 attempts occur each year. This means that there is one attempt every 38 seconds. There are approximately 25 attempts for each suicide death and 3 female attempts for each male attempt. Younger people make more attempts than older people; for older people who die by suicide, their first attempt often is the lethal one.

For more statistics related to these breakdowns, see the American Association of Suicidology web site *(www.suicidology.org)* and look under "Stats and Tools." For world statistics, search the World Health Organization web site (*www.who.int*) under "suicide."

The reality is that suicide is a problem and one that will not disappear on its own (or easily). It leaves loved ones devastated, trying to understand what they did wrong and feeling a loss of hope themselves. In the next section we will discuss some of the risk factors that lead to these statistics.

As it takes several years for data to be collected in the United States (all fifty states must report), and then deciphered and disseminated, at the time of the printing of this book, it is difficult to say exactly what the outcome of the world economic crisis will be on suicide rates for 2008 and beyond. What we do know is that calls to crisis centers are up and people are reaching out for help more than ever. Hopefully, existing resources will be marketed in such a way as to reach the people who need them, and new resources will be created to meet the demand.

Risk Factors

Suicide is hard to generalize about because it is so complicated. Behind each suicide is a story as unique as the person who died. Ultimately, we are left to decipher that story based on what we know about the person and who was left behind (called a psychological autopsy). That loved one took with him or her the actual reasons for ending a shortened life. I often tell people that if suicide were so easy to prevent, suicidologists could hand everyone a flyer and send them home. Instead, we spend hours discussing and learning what could be warning signs and risk factors and those hours are still not enough because we also must discuss how you help someone you are concerned about.

Suicide is not determined by one event. Most suicides occur after a series of events in one's life. The bereaved typically can look back on the history of a loved one and see a pattern and history leading up to the death.

Even though suicide is complicated and knows no boundaries, there are risk factors. In the United States, they include living in western states (isolation and access to firearms), mental illness, previous suicide attempt, previous loss, sexual orientation questioning, alcohol/drug abuse, stigma, poverty, being male, and having a family member who died by suicide.

Terminally ill people sometimes choose suicide as a means to end their pain rather than waiting out their time to die. Such decisions raise the question, If life is sacred, should we "be allowed" to end our own lives when we are terminal and/or in constant pain? This issue is not likely to be resolved any time soon (or ever). It is important to understand that, just as our politics vary from person to person, we have individual beliefs about how we end our lives, often related to religious inclination. My experience is that the people bereaved by these deaths often understand why their loved ones chose to end their lives on their terms and are in a different place than many other survivors of suicide loss. While they are sad that their loved one has died, they feel relieved that their pain has ended and they respect the decision that the loved one made.

In the United States, it appears that a high percentage of the people who die by suicide have a diagnosable mental disorder, although we currently have no way to track this data. A mental disorder could be anything from depression to bipolar disorder to schizophrenia. Many times mental disorders bring with them an array of other issues: substance abuse, relationship issues, and unemployment among others. While some people are getting help for their mental disorder, others have refused help and still others do not have access to it (or cannot afford it).

Even though women are more likely to attempt suicide, men are more likely to use lethal means that end in death, which makes being male a risk factor. Traditionally, much of the funding, particularly in the United States, has gone to support youth suicide prevention to avoid the tragedy of lives cut short. Youth suicide is the third leading cause of death for fifteen to twenty-four year olds, after accidents and homicides, as youth typically do not die of diseases and illnesses. (Suicide is the eleventh leading cause of death for all age groups, with the top ten comprising diseases and illnesses,particularly heart disease and cancer.) Unfortunately, putting the majority of funding into youth suicide has left an open wound for all the children and young people who are losing their fathers and male role models to suicide.

While it is often assumed that most suicides are related to mental disorders (like depression and substance abuse), the World Health Organization (2010) points out that this is not true in all countries. For instance, in Asian countries (and the United States), there is an impulsivity factor. It is imperative to keep cultural factors in mind when looking at risk factors. While guns are used by the majority of people who end their lives in the United States, in the world overall pesticides are the method of choice. Keeping the most lethal methods out of the hands of people who might use them to end their lives (also known as means restriction) is a key piece of any suicide prevention program. In some countries, pesticides are placed in locked boxes, and in the United Kingdom some medications are packaged so that lethal doses of over-the-counter painkillers cannot be purchased all in one container.

In the United States, environmental risk factors include living in the western states, as you probably noticed from reading the names of the five states with the highest rates of suicide. One factor in the high rate of suicide in the West is probably the number of people living in rural areas where mental health care is not as accessible or not available at all. Often, people who live remotely can be identified as more independent and could be less apt to reach out for help even when it is available to them. They also might be more likely to have access to firearms and to live in an environment where firearms are part of the culture (even for people who might have talked about suicide previously).

People who live alone are at a higher risk for suicide. They might not reach out for help because they are alone, and if they don't have regular contact with anyone it is less likely that someone will recognize any warning signs. Being unemployed and the ending of a marriage are also risk factors. Think of anything in a person's environment that might make him feel less hopeful and/or less able to ask for support.

Any sort of previous loss in one's life can be a risk factor for suicide. Many people who are reading this book are reading it because of a loss and understand that sense of longing for the physical presence of the loved one who is no longer here. Because society traditionally has not accepted the grief journey as one that should be processed and allowed to happen (think about how people traditionally receive several days of bereavement leave and then are expected to return to work and resume their lives), people who are grieving often do not feel they can reach out for help. They wonder what is wrong with them because they feel sad and miss their loved one when the rest of the world seems to be telling them to move on with their lives. What they do not realize is that it is a normal part of the journey and one that does not have to lead to hopelessness.

While there are ethnic groups that have higher rates of suicide, the GLBT (Gay Lesbian Bisexual Transgender) community also has a heightened risk for suicide. This is because of the confusion, stigma, and shame they feel about coming out about their sexuality. If someone is uncertain he (or she) will be accepted by family and loved ones because of his sexual identity, he is less likely to reach for help. For information and support for this group, see The Trevor Project (*www.thetrevorproject.org*) which offers a suicide and crisis prevention helpline for gay and questioning youth.

Family history of suicide is an important risk factor. There is some debate over the part that genetics play in suicide, but exposure to suicide is correlated with an increase in suicidal behavior by surviving family members. When suicide happens in a family, it becomes part of that family's history and the family's everyday language. It no longer is something that happens to a family down the street. Hence some family members might see suicide as a method of coping with stress.

Family history also can include violence and trauma. In families with a history of one or both (they usually come together, since where there is violence, there is trauma), for some family members the only escape might be to kill oneself. And in some families a single member has been exposed to war and violence (currently this is particularly true for active military and for veterans who have served in the conflicts in the Middle East).

While the risk factors described above do not encompass all people who are at risk for suicide (and there are people who fall into these categories but might not ever consider suicide), these people are the ones we generally believe are more likely to exhibit suicidal thoughts that lead to possible lethal attempts to end their lives.

There is much more to explore, much that we still do not understand about why people take their lives. An excellent book discussing the many varied reasons is *Why People Die by Suicide* by Thomas Joiner (see the resource section at the end of this book). Dr. Joiner, whose father died by suicide, goes through the many reasons people end their lives and how they reach that point.

Warning Signs

The signs of suicide, what a person might actually show prior to a suicide attempt, include behaviors that are not typical for the individual. They include depression, eating a lot/a little, sleeping a lot/a little, talking about suicide, and mood changes. The AAS provides a mnemonic created by a group of experts and researchers to help us remember what the warning signs of suicide are:

IS PATH WARM?

- **I** Ideation (thoughts of ending one's life/suicide)
- **S** Substance abuse
- **P** Purposelessness
- **A** Anxiety
- **T** Trapped
- **H** Hopelessness
- **W** Withdrawal
- **A** Anger
- **R** Recklessness
- **M** Mood Changes

It is important to ask a person if they are suicidal if you are concerned about them. There is no reason to fear asking; in fact many people feel much relief after someone has asked them. Asking someone if they are suicidal will not put the idea into the head of someone who has not already been thinking about suicide. But if you do ask, be prepared to help. Know the resources in your community to refer them to a trained clinician, or call the national number below.

If you are worried about someone you love, call the Suicide Prevention Lifeline at 1-800-273-TALK (8255). More information about helping suicidal people is available on the AAS web site as well.

History

Suicide has been part of life as long as there have been human beings. And it has quite a history. In some cultures it has been viewed as a heroic act or martyrdom (kamikazes in World War II, suicide bombers in today's society), while in other cultures and religions it has been considered a sin. At some points in history, families whose loved ones died by suicide were stripped of all their belongings and the loved one was not buried in a cemetery. In some cultures it is still a taboo to speak of a person who has died by suicide.

George Howe Colt, in his book *November of the Soul: The Enigma of Suicide* (see the resources section for more information), does a comprehensive job discussing the history of suicide and what it means. Also, author Lisa Lieberman in *Leaving You: The Cultural Meaning of Suicide* explains the history of suicide and the associated stigma and shame that endure to this day.

While the ultimate goal for all of us is to eradicate suicide, it might not be completely possible, and it would certainly take generations to change how people think, act, and react. However, there is definitely much room for supporting people. As Mickey Heilig, one of the founders of the field of suicidology, put it in September 2009, we have put much focus on discerning who is suicidal and not enough on treatment.

Protective Factors

Just as important as examining what puts people at risk for suicide, it is significant to point out some of the protective factors that guard against suicide. Some are simply opposites of the risk factors, such as access to mental health resources rather than barriers to mental health resources and being connected in a community rather than living alone in an isolated place. But protective factors also include feeling connected to society as a whole—for instance, having a sense of cultural and religious belonging. Coping and communication skills also are helpful. As the road of life is not an interstate highway where we can see for miles ahead of us, we need to know how to navigate the difficulties and barriers that we encounter.

The reality is that almost anyone is at risk for suicide. And suicide can affect any of our lives in the blink of an eye. What makes the grief experience difficult for many people who reflect on their loved one's life is that he or she might have been living a full life. Maybe on the outside the person did not appear to have many problems, or to have problems that could not be handled. But we do not always know what is swirling around in someone's mind. We might not know their true fears or their hesitancy to reach out for help.

Those of us left behind after a suicide have several choices. We can let the loss ultimately tear us apart, or make the better choice to go forward with our lives and use the loss of our loved one as a springboard for a new beginning. We do not leave them behind; they come with us as the story and the experience that we use to help ourselves and others.

3. The Suicide Grief Experience

The reality is that death is inevitable for all of us. It is inevitable that people and pets we care about will die at some point in our lives. And it is inevitable that we will die. But in our society, we treat death as if it is a faraway object, one not to be touched or talked about. It is as if by taking it off the shelf and examining it, we might get hurt.

But as much as we fear death, we also are curious about it. Think how many movies and books have death and loss as a theme; listing them would take a very long book. And how many times have we heard about sports stars whose achievements were motivated by the loss of someone they cared about?

I often hear and read how we need to "normalize" grief. The reality is that grief *is* normal. What is not normal is the way we treat it in our world. It is not something we should push aside or tell people to get over. Feeling sad and hurt because someone we care about has died is painful. And normal. By processing what we feel, we are allowing ourselves to grieve and to let it come naturally.

Grief is an individual road, though, which is part of the reason it often is something we prefer to read about as the experience of someone else. Because we do not give people some idea of what to expect after a loss, people fear it. But there is no right way to grieve. What works for one of us might not work for anyone else. Much of how we grieve comes from who we are—our personalities, our losses, our goals, and how we see the future. Grief does not have a timeline. Many factors, discussed throughout this book, will define how long and/or intense the grief experience might be for each of us.

Throughout our lives we have been told that our attitude is half the battle. Do we look at life as the glass half full or half empty? Do we see what is positive about an event or only the negative? The same can be said for the grief experience. Although it feels impossible, especially right after a loved one has died, to see grief in a positive light, we cannot turn back the clock and bring our loved one back. Do we see grief as something that is insurmountable and fear we will never be able to get past the sad feelings we have? Part of the reason for naming this book *Rocky Roads* is because grief can be looked upon as an adventure in some way. Obviously it is not an adventure any of us would have chosen but a road that can be treacherous and one where we can learn something about ourselves and become stronger people. Viewing grief as something we should attack head on (not all in one day, though!) will help us travel the road ahead.

Suicide grief, however, has a unique place among the emotions around death. Self-inflicted death is not considered a usual way for people to die. It is said that we should not end our lives, that it is not our choice to exercise nor should it be an option. That means that suicide grief often will not follow the normal patterns of a grief experience. It is a reality that some of us will face and the reason that most of you have picked up this book to read.

Suicide challenges us to rethink our values and our beliefs. Although it has been seventeen years since my sister died, I still can remember how at twenty-one years old I was forced to rethink everything I valued and believed after her suicide. It is as though everything is stripped away from us and we must build our lives anew. And because it takes time to rebuild, it also can take us longer to integrate the grief and everything that follows into our lives. That is one reason suicide grief can take longer to journey through than other types of mourning.

When someone dies from an illness, we often have a chance to prepare for the death. While the experience can vary in terms of how much the person dying is willing to discuss the end of his or her life, for the people who are present while the person is dying, there is an opportunity to begin the grief process (called anticipatory grief). There is still grief after the death but in some way we are already saying goodbye before the loved one dies and getting used to the idea that the loved one will not be around too many more days.

Things are different when someone dies in an accident, is murdered, or dies by suicide. There can be trauma because the events usually are unexpected. There is shock to cope with (see later section on shock in the reaction to the death) and the reality that the person's life has ended, usually without the surviving loved ones saying goodbye. With accidents and homicide there are unique issues: for accidents, that something went wrong; or for homicide, that another person ended the loved one's life purposely.

In suicide, of course, the issue is that the loved one has ended his or her own life. The loved one might leave a suicide note, although not all suicides leave notes (there is a range of opinion about how often suicide notes are left behind and what they say). Even a suicide note, though, does not give the surviving person a chance to speak any last words to the loved one. Part of the suicide grief experience is finding a way to do that without the person being physically present.

Homicide-suicide is a combination of the two events where a person will murder at least one other person (anyone from loved ones to people who just happened to be standing in the range of the person with the gun) and then him or herself. This also is called familicide. When this happens, it has its own set of issues for the people who must grieve multiple losses of family members at a parallel time. They also must cope with the possible legal issues from family members (like a spouse's family) and likely media coverage.

People often say that when someone dies by suicide they are "not in their right mind," but I do not believe that to be true for all people who die by suicide. While a large number might have some form of alcohol or drugs in their bodies when they die (thus lowering their inhibitions, which makes it easier to do things one normally does not do like end one's life), others plan their suicides, sometimes for weeks or even longer. I believe that was the case for my sister, whose suicide note was not dated. She also had plans to see me several weeks after the day when she died. In the years that I have had to reflect on her death and the time leading up to it, I believe the decision might even have been made two months before. Because of her bulimia, depression, and the date rape she endured, I believe she said, "I'm seventeen years old. What else can happen to me? I can live sixty more days but not sixty more years."

I bring this up because while she had planned her suicide, it was not known to us. It still was an unexpected event although she knew she was going to do it (right down to the night before her death when she made the joking comment about how I used to call my hair "my golden locks" which I believe now was her way of saying goodbye). Although she knew she was saying goodbye, I had no idea of the road that would roll out in front of me the next morning after she ended her life.

Who is a suicide survivor and how many of us are there?

Many questions surround the number of survivors left behind after a suicide. For years, the number six has been used to describe how many people are directly affected by the loss of a loved one to suicide. Is that number accurate, though?

In the 1950s the founder of suicidology, Edwin Shneidman, was asked to consult on a case where a cemetery had been double-burying bodies. When he was asked how many people in a family deserved a judgment, Shneidman replied six because he believed common sense dictated that compensation was owed to the immediate family. And so the number stuck (Linn-Gust, 2004). We say that at least six people are affected by a suicide loss.

Six will sound too low to anyone who is bereaved by suicide. In my immediate family, there were five of us (mom, dad, two siblings, me), and that does not count the extended family, her friends, our friends, neighbors, school community, and the many other people who today I still know were profoundly affected by her death. It may be many more—even hundreds.

The reason the number six does not reflect how many people are truly affected by a suicide is that blood and legal ties do not always describe the people left behind following a suicide. The following chapter will discuss how a family is defined. However, family members are not the only people who can be survivors of suicide. Frank Campbell, Julie Cerel, and the Baton Rouge Crisis Center found a long list of unique relations (over forty) who sought help after a loved one had died by suicide. Mothers led off the list followed by sister, wife, daughter, son, friend, and father (Cerel, 2010). In a random telephone survey conducted in Kentucky asking people if they knew someone who had died by suicide, the most common relationship category by far was friend (36.3 percent) followed by cousin (8.1 percent). These were followed by extended family, friend's family, uncle, co-worker, and acquaintance (Cerel, 2010). Clearly, people who are seeking help are close family members (and usually female), yet many people know someone who has lost a loved one to suicide or knows someone whose loved one died by suicide.

Even if not all these people are family members, they all are somehow affected by the suicide. For instance, someone like the maid who finds a deceased person in a motel room also is bereaved by suicide because she is somehow affected by that suicide (usually traumatized). While such a person might not realize she is a survivor, since she did not know the deceased, she has been affected nevertheless. Cases like this are part of the continuing debate about the bereaved by suicide.

Then there are the family members who might deny they are bereaved, who do not want to admit that their loved one died by suicide or that they were related to that person. They are bereaved because they obviously are affected by the death (although they will not admit it!).

For older people who live alone, their other family members might have died or live far away and the people closest to them might be their friends and neighbors (Harwood, et al., 2001). Often these people receive less support during grief even though they might be the only people to have had daily contact with the person who died by suicide.

Friends, classmates, and neighbors of any age often do not get support after a suicide loss but they are clearly bereaved because they most likely experienced the daily routine of life with the deceased (like having a discussion while taking the trash out in the evening). Often, the people in the routine of life are not considered bereaved because they are not relatives even when they knew more about the person who died than some family members.

By assuming six survivors are affected by each suicide loss, researcher John McIntosh, through the AAS, estimates that from 1982 to 2006, 4.6 million people became survivors of suicide. That means that one of every 65 Americans is bereaved by suicide and if there is a suicide every 15.8 minutes, there also are at least 6 new survivors every 15.8 minutes (McIntosh, 2009). However, as noted above, this impressive number is a gross underestimation of how many people are left behind after a suicide.

As we continue to ask the right questions, the hope is that we can better grasp these numbers through better estimations (Berman, in press).

Normal vs. Prolonged Suicide Grief

As we discussed in a previous chapter, grief is sadness we feel when we experience a loss. Obviously, each person's experience with grief will be unique. We are unique individuals and lead unique lives. Our relationships with our families and the deceased loved ones will be unique. We will talk later in this chapter about the different aspects of grief. But one question people often have is, "How do I know if my grief is normal? When should I get help?"

It is normal to miss someone you love, to be sad that they are gone, to long for their presence. A large portion of the grief experience, as mentioned in the introduction to this chapter, is simply allowing these emotions to flow. I describe grief as a journey because it is a process. A process, like a journey, is something that changes and evolves as we travel through it. Right now we might feel we cannot survive beyond the next five minutes, but in several months, we might be feeling good and then suddenly feel very sad. At some point the road will even out, but there still will be bumps. After all, it is a rocky road but one that is nevertheless passable.

For some people, though, the bumps in the road might not smooth out. They might still feel as if they cannot survive for five more minutes even though they have survived for days, weeks, months, and even years after the death. These bereaved people might be experiencing prolonged (formerly known as complicated) grief.

Prolonged grief consists of several aspects. In addition to continued yearning and searching for the loved one, it also encompasses four or more unrelenting symptoms of trauma that have come about because of the death (Prigerson et al., 1999). These symptoms include avoidance of reminders of the deceased; purposelessness; feelings of futility; difficulty imagining a life without the deceased; numbness; detachment; feeling stunned, dazed, or shocked; feeling that life is empty or meaningless; feeling as if a part of oneself has died; disbelief; excessive death-related anger or bitterness; and identification symptoms or harmful behaviors resembling those suffered by the decedent (Prigerson, et al., 1999).

People who show signs of complicated grief should seek professional help. While complicated grief can lead a person to thoughts of suicide (or even a suicide attempt), there is support for someone who needs that extra hand along the road. Grief should not hurt so deeply for such a long period of time. There is help for people who find themselves feeling swallowed up by the pain of their loss.

The Concept of Time

No one likes to be told that "grief will take time." However, the reality is that we measure events and experiences through the calendar. We talk about a day ago, a week ago, a year ago, and so on. We use time as a measurement and sometimes repeat the proverb "time heals all wounds." Even though we will find ourselves measuring our grief experience using the calendar, grief is on its own timeline. For instance, for some people, depending on how long the initial shock or numbness lasts, the second year of grief can be more difficult because that shock and numbness has worn off. But whether it specifically "hits" at the second year is a variable we cannot predict because each person's experience is unique.

Grief Rituals after Suicide

The stigma of suicide often has affected the immediate death rituals (funerals, memorials, services, wakes, viewings) after a suicide. Historically, for instance, because the Catholic Church would not allow any person who died by suicide to have a funeral mass or be buried in a Catholic (blessed) cemetery, if families could keep the secret of the death being a suicide, they did. Families were denied the Catholic rituals so important to them because of the nature of the loved one's death. This attitude has not disappeared, but it is not as prevalent as it used to be.

For some families, the stigma of suicide alone was enough to deter them from having a funeral. Sometimes loved ones were cremated before all the family members knew about the suicide. In the video documentary about her mother's death called *After a Suicide,* Diane Conn recounts that when her mother died, "We had no funeral. We didn't know how to mourn someone who chose to die."

The residues of these decisions affect families for years as other members of the family (particularly children) never were given a chance to say goodbye. These family members must eventually find some way to say goodbye. Funerals and the rituals that surround them are for the living.

All family members, including children, should be given the option of taking part in the planning of the rituals and attending rituals for the loved one who died. For instance, some children might be offered the opportunity to say something about their loved one. Even if they decline the offer, they still know there was an effort to include them. This might be helpful to them when they are older.

Chances are, by the time you pick up this book, the rituals are over. But if there were no rituals and you feel as though you were not given that chance to remember your loved one and to say goodbye, it does not mean you cannot do something. The ritual can be as simple as going to the cemetery and saying a prayer. It can be done by yourself or with other willing family members. Even though someone else might be struggling with having a ritual to say goodbye, no other family member's grief should be hindered by the choice of one member.

Stages vs. Tasks

There is debate about Elizabeth Kubler-Ross's Stages of Death and Dying (denial, anger, depression, bargaining, and acceptance), which often have been used to describe how people cope with grief (although the stages originally described those facing death in palliative care). When the stages are explained to people, they often say, "Well, I didn't go through all of those" or "I didn't go through them in that order." I do not believe Kubler-Ross meant that people travel through them all at the same time or in that order. Some people do not experience all of them. And no one stays in them for the same amount of time.

Just as *Rocky Roads* is a guide, concepts like the stages of dying or other theories explained here should be considered the same. They give a grieving person some idea what he or she might experience during the grieving process. Again, that all depends on the person, the type of death, and the relationship to the deceased. And just as there is an ongoing debate over the use of the term *suicide survivor*, people are questioning if the Kubler-Ross stages truly represent what we experience in grief and how we define ourselves after the loss.

Another approach to mapping the process is the Grief Task Theory by Therese Rando (1992–93), which defines the particular tasks one must go through following a loss, Although I do not believe they are always traveled through in this order (although one must accept the loss before moving forward on the healing journey) or that each person will travel through all of them, the theory describes some important pieces to grief.

- React to the separation
- Remember and re-experience the lost person and the relationship

Those first two stages easily describe part of the process of coping with loss. However, it is these next three stages that I think are just as significant on the grief journey.

- Give up the attachment to the person and the life that used to be

Often after the loss of a loved one, particularly after a suicide because of the nature of death, people fear giving up their attachment to the loved one. They are afraid that if they let go of any part of the attachment, the person will not be connected to them anymore. They also do not want to let go of the life that they used to have. Once the person dies, however, all lives connected to that person are irrevocably changed. People fear that by letting go they will also lose hold of their memories of their loved one. That is not the case though. I do not believe that we give up the attachment so much as we have a new attachment to that person (we must let go of the physical attachment to our loved ones yet we are still connected because they remain part of our lives but in a different way).

- Move into the new life but remember the old

Those who are moving into a new life do not let go of the old life. Often I have told people, you cannot let go of all the memories and time you shared with a loved one in days or even weeks. Those memories and the times you shared are yours to keep. You move forward, you laugh again, you experience life in a different way, but your loved one is still part of the past and who you are today. After all, without them, you wouldn't be who you are now.

- Reinvest emotions and energies in other relationships and activities

This is not bad. You have every right to enjoy life. Your loved one could not see beyond the pain. We do not forget our loved ones, but we do have choices to rekindle dying relationships or spark new ones. And we have opportunities to engage in new activities. Part of what grief is about is helping us learn about ourselves. We find strength we never thought we had. And we find interests and new people. The opportunities to make our lives more rich and satisfying are right there in front of us if we choose to grab them.

The Reaction

When we find out that a loved one has died,, it often feels like a rock has hit the windshield as we are driving along a road. It comes out of nowhere. We could be in the middle of a routine day, working through whatever we have to do on our daily list when we get the call. Or we find our loved one dead. Or we witness the act itself and rush to call emergency services. Whatever surrounds how we found out, it is the shock of the news that will see us through the next few weeks. Our life as we knew it grinds to a halt when a loved one dies by suicide. Suddenly, the routine is thrown away and life becomes simply getting through each day.

Chances are, by the time this book is in your hands, you are past those days and weeks. However, someone who cares about a family who is bereaved by suicide might be reading this book and wondering what it was like for the family immediately after the suicide.

The shock, which acts as a barrier to the news, helps us to absorb it in a way that works for each of us. We might have to sponge it up in small doses and then go to something else. Children, for example, might decide to play for awhile and act as if nothing has happened. This isn't true; they simply are digesting as much as their developing brains will allow them at one time. Some people might need to feel normal while other people are upset that they are watching television or knitting. Family members will continue throughout the grief process to question each other as members will be in different places of the grief process at different times.

In shock, we cannot believe what has transpired— that our loved one has died. And by suicide. It does not seem possible that we have been thrust onto this road of grief. We yearn to reach back in time and change what happened. Maybe if we had stopped them from leaving or talked to them. Anything. What did we miss?

There is such a thing as expected shock (Maple, et al., 2007). In expected shock, the bereaved knew that at some point the person was going to die by suicide; it was just a matter of when the suicide would happen. In other cases, we realize the possibility always was there. That might be difficult to admit. Because many people who die by suicide are mentally ill (whether diagnosed or undiagnosed), life with them might have been difficult. They previously might have threatened suicide or attempted to kill themselves.

Slowly, we will adapt to the reality that our loved one has died. Sometimes this is made easier by the rituals that surround the death of a loved one. We might have a wake/viewing, a funeral, or a memorial service. The rituals are not about the person who died, they are about us having the opportunity to say goodbye. And it is a time to reflect on the life of the loved one. The hope is that you will let go of the way your loved one died and be able to remember them for who they were in life. But the only place to get there is to trudge down this road called grief.

The Emotions

There are many emotions wrapped up in grief. And each of us experiences them differently from other members of our families. We all have to understand that these differences are common, and by understanding what another person is enduring, family members can take a step back and allow that person to ride the wave of a particular emotion. While grief sometimes has been classified in stages, the reality is that it's hard to place people in boxes. We are all unique. That means our grief also is going to be unique.

Denial While denial can be part of the shock of the initial reaction after the loved one has died, it also takes time for someone to accept that a loved one has died, and has died by suicide. However, if the denial continues months and years after the death, it can become a problem and part of complicated grief (discussed previously in this chapter). Initially, however, we all experience a shock when someone we love has ended his or her life. It is understandable to deny what has happened. We want so badly to return to the day or weeks before, when life was different. However, when we continue to deny (or a loved one continues to deny) that the person died or died by suicide, it is important that we help them find support for that acceptance.

Sadness Obviously in grief we will experience sadness. We have to mourn for the loved one who has left us. We have to mourn for the past we cannot share with them anymore. And we have to mourn for the future we will not share. And we mourn for ourselves that we have to go forward. Sadness is to be expected. It is natural.

But it is also somewhat out of our control. It might take us some time to get up the nerve to do things that were part of our routine lives before the person died, but now seem like huge hurdles. Iris Bolton, author of one of the first books written by a survivor, about her son's death (see Resources), sometimes tells the story in her workshops about a trip to the grocery store. She was doing fine, gathering the things the family needed. But when she reached the cereal aisle and saw her son Mitch's favorite cereal, she broke down at the reality that her son was dead and she would not be buying that cereal again because he would not be there to eat it. Iris ended up fleeing the grocery store, leaving her filled cart in an aisle because the sadness and the emotions of her loss overwhelmed her.

She is not unique. Some people are afraid to leave the house because they might break down. The reality is that loss is part of life and maybe not suicide loss, but loss itself, happens to all of us. I have found support in the most unusual places, and it is because I have allowed myself to let the sadness flow naturally as it should. It is natural to feel sad that our loved one is gone. So we must let the tears fall when they need to. And if we do that, the tears will subside in time and be replaced by the happy memories of life with our loved one.

What is not okay is when the sadness turns to a depression that we cannot shake (or we refuse to seek help for). While we might not be suicidal or even thinking about suicide, we still cannot get out of bed and find we are losing hope in our lives. The chapter on suicide listed the signs of depression, but it is most important to pay attention to behaviors that are not like our normal patterns. This is not a usual time in our lives: grief is not something that we consider routine like picking up the newspaper on our front lawn in the morning, but it also is not meant to make us so depressed that our loved ones are worrying about us. When that happens, it is time to seek help, through a therapist, someone who can act as a guide for a survivor of suicide loss (we will discuss how and when to find one in a later chapter).

Shame and Stigma Several emotions typically related to suicide can overwhelm people during grief. The first is shame because of the stigma of suicide. We discussed in the previous chapter how shame and stigma are intertwined with suicide and have been for a long time. I believe this is one of the key places in suicide grief where people need help. If we did not feel so ashamed of how our loved one died, I do not believe this book would be needed nor would I be out speaking about suicide grief. But the shame and stigma complicate grief, a process that already is difficult because our society has a tendency to brush death under the rug. Not only is suicide brushed under the rug, but the rug is then hidden in another room with the door shut.

We feel ashamed because our loved one did something that is not looked favorably upon by others in society. We are afraid to reach out for help because we feel stigmatized. Shneidman said that people who kill themselves leave psychological skeletons in the emotional closets of the people who are bereaved by the suicide (Cain, 1972). He was right. Somehow we have to open up the closet and take those skeletons out and acknowledge them. There is no reason to be ashamed or stigmatized by the way our loved one died. We did not make that choice for them. Obviously, no one wants that for a loved one. And if we had any say in it, they would still be here with us.

Even the media still stigmatize suicide. Think of television shows and movies that either glorify suicide or show it as a crime. They continue to use the word *commit*. It all adds up.

Our degree of stigma and shame can be affected by how we are treated by first responders after the suicide—the police, the medical investigator, the doctors, and/or anyone else who might be involved in the end of our loved one's life. I have heard of instances where a loved one shot him or herself at home and other members of the family were immediately taken away by the police for questioning, in case the death was a homicide. People have talked of not being treated kindly or in a comforting way by the police or medical investigator because the death was clearly a suicide. Doctors might not be sympathetic because the person overdosed. Educating first responders is the mission of some bereaved people who want to make sure other people will be treated better than they were. Often, the first responders simply do not know how to treat the families.

In Baton Rouge, Louisiana, Frank Campbell, in conjunction with the Baton Rouge Crisis and Intervention Center has created LOSS Teams (Local Outreach to Suicide Survivors) which train the bereaved to travel with the medical investigator (the coroner in some places) after the suicide to comfort the family. More of these teams are being formed around the world. They create a sense of caring after the suicide as well as outreach for the people trying to comprehend the loss of a loved one by suicide. (More information on Frank and the LOSS Teams can be found at *www.lossteam.com*). For many survivors, meeting a LOSS team or similar group can make the difference between fearing the shame and stigma communicated by the first responder and reaching out for help and not allowing the shame and stigma to rule the suicide grief experience. It also educates the bereaved on helpful resources in the local community.

Shame and stigma are self-inflicted to some extent. We allow people to trap us there. We do not have to. Our loved one was an important part of our lives and remains so. In time, I believe, society will move away from shame and stigma, but it is up to us to make that happen by being open about how our loved ones died and not allowing people to make us feel bad for what we have been through.

When I look at the group of people who we consider the pioneers of the bereaved by suicide movement here in the United States, the people who paved the way so that I could be here today doing the work that I do, I look at how much stigma they faced. Many of them lost children in the late 1970s and early 1980s (several lost parents and siblings). There were no support groups and so few resources.

And then I look at the new faces, including my own, of the next generation of the movement, how we have not had to face that same agonizing stigma. But as Heidi Bryan, a fellow sibling survivor, once pointed out to me, perhaps we also just do not care. We are younger and times have changed, so we have a different attitude. For whatever reason, we have come a long way and we continue to trudge forward so that future bereaved do not have to cope with what we have been through.

Guilt and Relief The other emotion that is really difficult for the bereaved in suicide loss is guilt. The could have, would have, should have. But before we discuss guilt more, it is important to touch on relief.

In families whose loved one has been sick for a long time, family life might have revolved around the loved one. Maybe there were late night calls from the police. Multiple trips to the psychiatric hospital. A lot of pain, fear, and trouble. Nothing in that family was routine since the onset of the illness (which could have been long before the family formed, which means nothing was ever routine in the family).

When the loved one dies, there is a sense of relief. There is a sense that life can be routine, especially for children who might have feared what was next and who only wanted to know that everything would be okay. But mostly, there is the feeling that they do not have to worry about the loved one because their pain is over. They will not suffer anymore.

Although my sister Denise did not have any prolonged mental illness (so far as we knew, since she was only seventeen when she died), Mom made the comment after she died that she did not have to worry about Denise anymore. For a parent, coping with a child who is depressed, bulimic, and has attempted suicide is a lot to deal with, especially when the child is only in high school. Would it have been worse in college when the child was away from home? Or would she have gotten through the rough patch and continued on with her life? Obviously, we will never know the answer. But we do know that everything that hurt her, including the date rape, would not hurt her anymore after she died.

Yet with that relief comes the guilt. The guilt for feeling relieved that a life has been ended, and ended through suicide.

Guilt can take over and not let go although I believe much of the reason we feel guilty is because our entire lives people have tried to make us feel that way. Guilt is like a monster that follows us around. And in suicide grief guilt is definitely a predominant emotion.

After all, what is there not to feel guilty about? Our loved one died by suicide. How does that make us look? We wonder what we did wrong partly because we believe the shame and stigma will make everyone question us and wonder what we missed or what we did not do to help our loved one. We believe people will question our family and think something is wrong with it. The bereaved replay events, any events that included the loved one. Mothers worry they let their child cry too long, siblings think they killed their brother by wishing he was dead when they were young, and spouses wonder if they did not show their husbands/wives they loved them enough. Every person can think of something that he or she could have done differently. We do not get any "do-overs" in life, and we do not know that if we had done things differently the outcome would have been different.

Part of what makes guilt complicated (and prevalent) in suicide grief is that we truly never will know why our loved one died by suicide. We will not know what ultimately led to the decision. And we wonder if we could have changed that outcome and how. So we run circles in our heads, telling the story of our loved one to anyone who will listen, looking for clues to help us understand what happened. But when we do not find that, we continue to beat ourselves up because that is what we've been taught to do. It is no different than the "Eat your green beans because there are starving children in Africa" that many of us grew up hearing. We were taught to feel guilty because all the starving children in Africa did not get green beans and therefore we should eat them. Because we did not do something, although we do not know what, our loved one died.

It is a huge step forward in suicide grief when bereaved people are able to let go of their guilt and realize they did everything they could. Until people can work through the guilt, they remain stuck in the guilt vortex. In their minds they cannot let go. Somehow, they need to find that place where they realize they did the best they could to keep their loved one alive.

Feelings of Failure After a suicide, several specific feelings of failure often haunt the bereaved. One is that they failed to keep the person on earth and wanting to live. Another is that they failed to protect the person from the method they used to kill themselves, drugs/alcohol, and/or anything else. They also might believe they failed to tell them how much they loved them and how important they were in their lives. Many of these feelings of failure lead people to guilt.

Anger Anger is common in suicide grief. After all, what is there not to be angry about? Our loved one died. They did not consult us and ask us if we were okay with it. They did not ask us if we could help them cope with life or the issues they felt surrounded them. Our lives have changed beyond our control. We did not ask to have to create a new normal. We did not ask to turn onto this road of grief. We did not ask for our family unit to be changed and complicated by the death of one of its members.

The most important part about anger is finding a way to release it so that it does not consume us. Anger can make us physically sick, it can sever relationships in our families, and it can make us do things we never thought we would do. Anger is not bad—it is all part of the grief process—but we need to keep it in check by finding ways to release it that do not hurt us or anyone else. This can be done by talking with people who will listen and help us process our emotions or it can be done by writing a letter to our deceased loved one. Finally, we can cope with anger by finding a physical release that allows us to let it go without hurting ourselves or others. There has been enough hurt after a loved one has died by suicide. It is not necessary to add more. I think of activities like going for a walk or run or even chopping wood. Some way to release that pain. (We discuss more ways to cope with our emotions and pain in a later chapter on coping.)

Blame I believe it is human nature to find something or someone to blame. Whenever we don't like the outcome of an event, we think of what or who we can blame for it going wrong. It makes sense to us in the maze of grief where we look anywhere for answers, even when they do not quite add up.

In the case of suicide, the most obvious blame target is the person who died. But some survivors will say they can never blame that person. Instead, they turn the blame on themselves or someone else. When people blame themselves, they are feeling guilty. But often when they blame others, the blame induces anger. And many times the blame and anger fall upon people in our own families.

Anyone can come up with a list of reasons for blame longer than this book. Ultimately, though, people are blamed for not being there for the deceased loved one. And this might not even be true. Someone does not know where to put his or her emotions and finds someone or something to lash out at. Blame is not healthy and we need to look inside ourselves and see why we feel the need to toss blame onto others.

Trauma Suicide grief often is associated with trauma. It can be traumatic because the bereaved person found the body, it can be traumatic because of the events that preceded the death, or it can be traumatic because of the events that followed the death. Whatever the reason for the trauma, it is part of the road one must travel following a suicide loss. If the trauma of the loss itself feels overwhelming and insurmountable (perhaps like the complicated grief described earlier) even after the shock has worn off, please seek help from a trained clinician and let him or her help you process your trauma. No one should be in that much pain following a suicide.

Physical Symptoms One aspect of the grief experience that we typically do not discuss is the physical symptoms. We have a tendency to think of grief as purely emotional, just as we usually consider illness physical rather than emotional. We treat the part that aches but do not realize that all parts of us, emotional and physical, work together. Grief is not only emotional but it is physical as well. It makes us tired. It saps our energy. It makes us not want to get out of bed. And it can make us sick, especially when we do not cope with it emotionally. Somehow it needs to find a place to come out, and it will emerge physically if it is not allowed to do so emotionally (and it is much harder on us physically than emotionally). I have met people who did not cope with their loss emotionally (usually by denying what happened to them, even after the shock wore off) and found themselves faced with physical ailments that were much worse than the emotions of grief ever could be.

We also need to take care of our physical selves during grief. We must sleep, and we need to eat right. We still should exercise. We will discuss more of these ways of caring for ourselves in the chapter on coping.

The Whys?

Suicide grief leaves behind a truckload of "Whys?" Probably the first statement out of our mouths after finding out a loved one died by suicide was "Why?" We will run circles around ourselves and everyone we know, wanting to know why our loved ones ended their lives. The reality is, though, that we never will truly know why because they took that answer with them.

After seventeen years, I can tell you that I have a pretty good idea of why Denise walked in front of that train. I know she was depressed, bulimic, and then she was date raped by a boy she knew. She was seventeen years old, and that is a whole lot of stuff to be coping with at a young age. I asked the why question over and over and over. We had several other theories (like the Prozac caused her to do it although that did not pan out since there was no Prozac in her blood when she died). At some point, I realized that while I could never fully shut the door on the why, partially because it appears that there was a suicide pact involved and at least one other girl knew about Denise's intent to die (none of them attempted suicide and none of them got Denise help either). I spoke to one of the girls in the early years after Denise's death but not the other one. She has been silent. There is nothing else I can find out about Denise's death. If she were here with me while I am typing this paragraph, she might say, "Oh no, you got it all wrong." With all the information that I have, it appears to me her pain was too great to continue forward. At such a young age, she only could see about a foot in front of her, and that is not very far.

Are people bereaved by suicide more at risk for suicide? There is research to support the notion that suicide runs in families (Runeson & Asberg, 2003). While genetics may have something to do with this, it is important to realize that when a suicide happens in a family, it becomes part of each member's vocabulary in a close and personal way. Suicide suddenly becomes an option. It happened once; therefore, it can happen again. Earlier in this book, we listed risk factors for suicide, and one of them was a previous loss. Just as for the suicidal person a previous attempt makes suicide more "normal," more a part of one's world, so does suicide itself.

Until my sister died, suicide was something that happened to the family down the street or on the Tuesday night movie. But once Denise killed herself, the reality for me was that if it happened once, it could happen again. Suddenly, my view of the world had changed, my sense of what was normal was gone, and everything I believed in was shaken. It was like one of those snow globes. Someone had shaken the one I was in, and it was a test of my strength to see if I could survive all the falling flakes and find status quo again.

While some family members profess that they would never kill themselves because they would not want to put the other family members through another suicide, others might really want to reconnect with the deceased loved one as part of trying to process what happened to the loved one who died.

Some survivors, particularly those who are younger than the one who died by suicide, fear that their own lives will end via suicide as was true for their sibling or parent. They will dread reaching the age of that person, wondering if it will happen to them, too.

Suicide becomes a part of a bereaved's family history and what we call the legacy of suicide. We must take care of the survivors left behind because postvention is prevention for the next generation. The only way to crack the cycle in families is to take care of the bereaved and support them through their losses so that they may find hope again.

The Reactions of Others

It is disappointing when people we care about, or believe will be there for us when a loved one dies, are not helpful. One of the most difficult lessons during suicide grief is that not everyone is willing to walk the road with us. People are uncomfortable with death, much less suicide. These people could be family members, friends, neighbors, doctors, clergy, and many other people who have been part of our lives and/or the life of our loved one who has died by suicide. The suicide grief experience is a lesson in who our true friends are.

We cannot predict how others will react. Because suicide is not something that we typically discuss with people (unless we have been personally affected by it), we do not know who is afraid of it, who has had experience with it (whether as an attempter or with one's family/friends), or who simply does not want to cope with it because of the sadness.

But what we do find out is who really wants to help us (and has the skills to help). Friends we did not realize cared that much about us are the ones who make the phone calls and bring us dinner. They are the ones who ask us months and years later how we are doing. And, along the way, we make new friends. Some of them are fellow bereaved while others are people who simply understand compassion. If suicide is to teach us to live life to the fullest, these are the people we find we want to surround ourselves with as we journey through grief. They are the ones accompanying us on the road.

While it is disappointing to watch people who exit our lives at the suicide, it is true that with each door or window that closes, a new one opens, out steps a new person, and this one will be there for the duration of the grief journey.

Culture, Religion, and Suicide

Knowing something about culture and religion is important in helping someone cope with a suicide death. Families can react differently to a suicide because of culture. We also can learn new ways of coping from other cultures. Culture can help people cope with loss, especially if it binds them historically to a place or group of people where they believe they belong.

Culture includes the values, beliefs, and traditions of a particular social, ethnic, or age group. We all are part of at least one culture, maybe more. Our families belong to a culture. We learn about life through our culture. It is often a way we identify ourselves and society. As for religion, it serves as community and also a footprint for us to follow in how to live our lives. Due to space limitations we cannot discuss all religions and cultures but if you are interested in how your religion or culture views suicide, it is best to talk with a clergy person, an elder, or someone else who can tell you more about it. If you are interested in how another culture views suicide, then consult someone in your region or community who can help you.

Particular to suicide, religion and culture can serve as both risk and protective factors. Many cultures and religions have stances on suicide that can sustain suicidal people with strong beliefs. Although they want to end their lives, if they believe that the end result for them will not be the outcome they want (going to hell or an undesirable afterlife rather than the paradise of a heaven), they may instead choose life. This is why some cultures have traditionally had lower suicide rates than others.

However, for the bereaved who are left behind after a suicide, such a culture makes their grief much more difficult to work through. If suicide is frowned upon and it is believed that the person has altered the natural course of his or her life, the family suffers in silence, afraid to talk about their loss and living in fear of exposure.

Also, some bereaved have been brought up with conflicting cultural and religious viewpoints. Their parents from different backgrounds came together to create another person who ultimately might not be sure which culture or religion he or she belongs to. An example of this might be someone who comes from two different Native American tribes that have differing perspectives on suicide. Or it could be that a Native American person lives in the dominant culture while his or her family is from a reservation. As a result he or she has one foot in each culture, not really sure where he or she belongs.

Often, culture, ethnicity, and religion are deeply connected. We must keep that in mind when we work with suicide survivors. Sometimes, we can mistake what we think are grief issues for what is really a culture issue. Never guess what someone believes!

One religion that we often hear about in regard to suicide is Catholicism, the religion in which I was raised. People understand that Catholics view suicide as a sin and that someone who dies by suicide will go somewhere less desirable than Heaven. For the bereaved, this makes for a difficult grief journey. However, what many people do not know is that the church changed its perspective on suicide in the new Catechism, published in 1994. The church no longer looks down on people who die by suicide and instead prays for them. This view will probably take hold slowly. The older generations (including the older priests) still hold that people go to that less desirable place after dying by suicide, and they still pass that attitude down to the next generation, and the cycle continues.

The example of Roman Catholicism shows how culture can be generational. What might be stigma laden in one generation might not affect the next. I think of some of the Native American tribes whose older members still live in isolation on the reservation. The younger members often have left the reservation for school and jobs. In the process, their beliefs about the suicide loss of a loved one might have changed. They might be more open to talking about the person they loved who has died by suicide but when they return to the reservation and to the elders they are not allowed to speak about that person. Parts of a culture may remain the same, while other parts change as the younger generations develop and integrate their nontraditional lives into the culture they come from.

When working with families of a culture or religion that is different from ours, we need to take the time to ask about their backgrounds. If we do not feel comfortable discussing such matters, we should at least do some reading on their beliefs and traditions because those also can be strengths for families. At that same time, we should remember that family members may not agree with all the beliefs of their background, or may come from more than one culture. Finding out from them what they believe is the best way to understand their view of suicide, death, and grief. We cannot change anyone's beliefs to mirror ours nor do we want to. By learning about another perspective on grief, though, we might learn something new that can help us with the losses that we encounter in our own lives.

Past Losses

As we process the loss of a loved one by suicide, it is important to acknowledge how past losses (by suicide or other modes of death) will affect the grief experience of this loss. Some people will have past losses, although maybe not by suicide, while for others, this will be the first death they will cope with of any kind in their lives.

For me, several of my grandparents had died before Denise, but their deaths did not leave me with the intense longing to turn back the clock and have the departed still part of my life. While I was sad, I realized that they had lived long, full lives and it was time for them to move on. But since Denise died, each death takes me back to her death, and that loss defines my grief experience in some way. I also look at grief differently with each loss because I seem to examine it in a new way compared to the previous experience.

As each person who dies in our lives had a unique relationship with us, so will that grief experience be unique. For people who experience more than one suicide in their lives, the past loss or losses will serve as a template for the grief experience ahead. We often look back on the grief experience and are amazed that we have traveled as far as we have. But when we have another loss, especially one as traumatic as a suicide loss, we feel ourselves stuck on the road. It is as if we are embarking on a long car ride and dreading the road in front of us. Yes, there will be similarities in the journey, but because our relationships with each person in our lives are unique, we cannot expect them to be the same. And while we might be dreading the road, it is important to remember that we have survived a past loss and we can survive this one, too.

Loss also leaves an imprint on our futures. However, that imprint does not have to be negative. Instead the relationship with the deceased loved one can be a guiding force for living our lives to the fullest and in the most fulfilled way possible.

Ultimately, grief leaves what feels like a gaping hole inside us. When we experience a loss, we have to reach deep inside ourselves to fill that hole and find hope again. In the depths of grief, immediately after the person dies, it feels like nothing/no one could ever replace that person. But we are not looking to replace that person. Mostly we are trying to understand what we are going through and why we are experiencing such confusing emotions before we can think about refilling the hole. We want to know how the hole got there and how we can fill it back up. With some understanding of the individual suicide grief experience, we can then think about how our families process the loss.

THE FAMILY

4. Introduction: Families and Suicide

This book is not meant to help you decide whom to blame in a family. The reality is that no family is perfect. Nor is any individual. Life is a series of lessons to be learned, and we all do the best we can with the skills we have at the time.

It would be easy to go through all the issues and problems a family could have had prior to the suicide, but the reality is that every family struggles in some way. I do not believe that in a book like this we should devote time to looking back on the family and assigning blame. While it is important to look back and process what we have been through in our families, holding onto that anger and disappointment does not help us move forward.

I do not believe that most people act out maliciously to other family members. Usually acting out is related to the person who is acting out, not to the recipient. Someone is angry or disappointed with himself or herself and turns that emotion toward others. This is not right but, again, this book is not about discussing why a person might have died by suicide. It is about acknowledging what happened and going forward to make the family stronger and help everyone to cope with the loss.

A family is constantly is growing and changing. The ultimate goal for parents when they start a family is to create independent, loving people who can leave the nest to create lives and families of their own. Look at a family photograph album. Through the years the outfits, the hairstyles, and furniture will change just as the family members grow and develop. While we might laugh at the outdated curtains and the funny clothes, the reality is that we want to see change happen in families. If the family is not changing, it is not growing and developing.

A suicide in the family can be a foreign event, and that is probably true for the majority of families who experience one. While there might be a family member in the past (great uncle, grandfather, cousin, etc.) who died by suicide, typically the suicide that led to reading this book is not an event that family members would have predicted in a million years. These families might need extra help because the knowledge of suicide is at a bare minimum ("Well, I once knew someone who lost someone to suicide..."). They need to understand why suicide happens and what suicide grief is about to cope with the suicide as individuals and as a family.

For other families, suicide is not the sole event. There has been other chaos in the family. It might not have been death (or it could have been death) but there might be other losses (divorce, jobs, homes). There could be abuse or other violent behavior. Mental illness. These families need help coping with the chaos that came before the suicide to keep future chaos at a minimum. They typically need outside help although it can be difficult to get all members to seek help.

5. What Is a Family?

To say someone is "family" is a tricky statement. Families are as unique as individuals. Defining the family in today's world is difficult because it can have such a wide range of meanings. What we called the traditional or nuclear family for many years does not exist as it used to. Families are not just mom, dad, and two kids. Instead, there are single-parent households, households where what we often called extended family (grandparents, aunts, uncles, cousins) live with a nuclear family, same-sex parent households, grandparents raising children, and the list goes on.

While there are several ways that families might be described, it ultimately is about how they describe themselves. What defines one family in one culture might be different in another. In some cultures (like the Navajo culture) someone might talk about a brother who someone in another culture would call a cousin. Some people are bound by DNA and blood while others do not feel they are a part of a biological family but have instead found people elsewhere in their lives who are more important to them than their DNA-related relatives. And people have friends they call family.

For some families, there is a sense of shared resources beyond the simple biological connection. It could be psychological (healthy or unhealthy) or financial. People also might define family as those to whom they are most attached and feel most connected. A group of people might consider themselves a family because they live in one dwelling. They may live under one roof for economic reasons, or because that is what they do culturally. Someone might be living with a family because that person has no other family or place to go. And pets are considered members of the family more today than ever.

Beyond the people we call family whose lives are intertwined with ours, typically on a daily basis, we also have other communities in our lives we might call family. We could have a church family, a work family, or a neighborhood family. We might rely on each of these families for different kinds of support. Our church family helps us spiritually as well as giving us a social outlet at least once a week; our work family helps us through daily trials; and a neighborhood family is there for us to help watch our kids and loan us that egg when we need one more to bake a batch of cookies.

6. The Family as a System

Families have been described as mobiles. When one member of the family leaves the others (in this case, by death), the entire family is thrown off, just as a mobile is when one piece is removed. The balance no longer exists. In the introduction to this book, I explained how LaRita Archibald struggled to cut a pie for her family in six pieces rather than seven after her son Kent died by suicide. In that sense, the Archibald family system became lopsided after Kent died. While he was no longer a part of the family in a physical sense, his death obviously still affected the family.

All families are in the same position after a suicide. The person still affects how the family reacts and the decisions they make. And there are choices to be made about how the family members grieve and move forward. The bond with this person is not broken when they die. It is important that the family acknowledge this, because families that do not acknowledge the ongoing bond will struggle to move forward. Without that acknowledgment, it seems, they cannot. It is not easy for a family to reach this point in the road either because family is a collection of different people. Some family members may want to deny the person was part of the family (possibly because the suicide is difficult to accept or because they hurt so much from the loss they are not sure how else to cope) while others cling to their memories of the person. Helping a family cope will be discussed in a later chapter.

A family always is trying to keep equilibrium, to keep that mobile balanced. But during the grief experience, the system goes through a transformation, one that will be both predictable and accidental (Bloch, 1991). Practical transformations might be changes because of a financial situation but usually constitute alterations in roles, particularly after the death of a parent. Accidental changes happen without the family realizing them, and they too can be positive or negative. Some of these changes happen because family members do not realize that their experience in grief is influenced by others and they in turn influence their relatives. In that sense, family members can hinder and/or help each other.

Within every family system, boundaries and rules govern how the family functions. Keep in mind that these boundaries and rules are unique to each family. However, they also can be culturally determined. Communication occurs in different ways in different cultures. When exploring a family's system, be sure to be aware of its culture.

Usually when we think of communication, we think of speech, but speaking is just one of the ways we get our thoughts across to one another. We also write them down. And we engage in nonverbal communication where our actions speak for us. In family systems, communication is how information is given to each family member. And it is not always kind, particularly after a suicide death. While some family members are angry, sadness prevails for others, and people tune each other out —or stop communicating. Somehow a family will have to come to an agreement about how they will communicate through the grief journey. It is through communication in the family system that we learn how to grieve. For example, children sometimes think they are not supposed to grieve (show that they are upset by the loss) because their parents do not let them see their grief.

Subsystems

Within the family, there are subsystems. There are the smaller relationships that exist within the family unit (also called dyads). They can include (but are not limited to) the parent-parent relationship, the siblings' relationships with each other, and the parents' relationship with each of their children. When other family members exist in the unit, their relationships with the respective members are included as well. These smaller systems have their own boundaries and rules.

When a suicide occurs in the family, the subsystems can change as the main family system has changed. While the family will never again exist in its former form, this is not bad. It simply means that the family as it once existed does not exist now. But everyone still has the right and opportunity to have a happy and full life. There is opportunity within the new subsystems for family members who might not have been close before to get to know each other and enjoy each other.

Because of the age difference between the siblings and the parents, different perspectives on stigma and awareness can drive a wedge in those relationships. The siblings are younger than the parents and might not feel the stigma around suicide as much as the parents do. The siblings might feel stifled by the lack of communication about the death being a suicide. If that happens, they will have to reach outside the family system for help.

Suprasystems

The environment outside the family is the suprasystem. It is the system that is larger than the family system. This includes the community that surrounds the family and also encompasses political and economic systems. The suprasystem can be the family's neighborhood or the town where it lives. It also can be cultural (for a Native American family it could be the pueblo or the reservation where they live) or related to a faith community. People in the military have the military community or base as a suprasystem.

People within a suprasystem are affected by the suicide.Often, however, they do not feel acknowledged because the focus is typically on the immediate family, and non family members may be afraid to reach out for support, or to reach toward the family for recognition of their pain. If they reach out to the family and the door is shut, they may take this to mean that their loss is not acknowledged even though the likelihood is that the members of the immediate family system are too ashamed or embarrassed to respond.

Suprasystems can change after a suicide. There are communities that no longer stay a part of the family's systems because the loved one has ceased being a part of them. They might remain a part of the suprasystems for some time after the death while the particular community grieves the loss, but at some point, they will fade away. A sports team that the deceased played on is an example of such a community. And of course if the family moves away because the loss changes the family's income and/or lifestyle, the surrounding community will change as well.

Families have boundaries (although some families have very loose boundaries). Boundaries define membership in the system and serve as a point of contact between the system and the other systems around it and inside it. These boundaries guard the information that comes into the family and goes out. In an alcoholic family, for example, the children are told to trust no one outside the family. But if nothing is let in or out, the family will break down. Families need new ideas. And they need support.

After the suicide, some families will let information and help into the family while others will close the door (sometimes because of embarrassment and sometimes as a coping mechanism). Families that allow their boundaries to remain somewhat permeable may find that support can reach them. It is also possible, though, for boundaries to be too loose. Allowing too many people access to the family is like having too many cooks in the kitchen; it helps to have one person take a leadership role in this situation. It may not be a family member, as the family members may simply not be able to do that. However, it should be someone the family trusts.

What works best is for families to have some boundaries, not too tight and not too loose. Again, the image of the mobile can help us to understand. How does a family achieve that balance without upsetting one part or another of the system, especially as one member is not physically part of the system anymore?

Support for suicide loss, while still limited, is more available today than it was just ten years ago. The hope is that a family will allow its boundaries to stay open, increasing the likelihood that support can make it into the system. Families that shut down may believe that shutting down is the best way to cope. Some members of the family may believe that the outside world is the reason the person killed him or herself. They might fear what others will say about them if they open their boundaries.

What they often forget is that there are members of the family who need help beyond the family unit. Children (of all ages) need their friends. Adults need the support of their extended family and of the outside community. While families need to be there for each other and to help each other, they also need the support of people outside the immediate family unit. The person who keeps the boundaries closed is keeping the other members from processing their grief, and this person is doing it because he or she is scared or embarrassed.

There also is a hierarchy in the system. Just as boundaries are important, so is the hierarchy. Too strict and the mobile is confined, too loose and it once again cannot stay balanced. Typically the parents are the hierarchy. Sometimes after a suicide, though, the hierarchy might appear to swing toward the children, as in situations where the children are parenting the parents because the parents are absorbed in their grief. We will discuss this more when we talk about how families grieve.

Finally, each person has a role within the family system. Those roles vary in families, but when one person dies, the roles in the family must shift. No one ever will be able to take over the role of the person who died. Instead, the roles of the other family members will change to some extent. The deceased person's place in the family, and all that she or he contributed (whether positive or negative), will be different in the family as the family has changed because of the death. If the leader of the family was the one who died, somehow the family will need to find new "glue" to hold the system together and support to keep the system in balance. This can take a long time.

A system is never stable; it always is changing and moving. Feedback travels back and forth through the family, affecting how the family moves. Each move that a family member makes and each piece of communication will affect the other members of the system. The family is not linear; it is a circular unit in which what each person does affects the other members of the unit. The family also affects the larger system around it by how it reacts to what comes in and out of it.

In grief, it is important for information to flow in and out of the system because resources need to come into it. An example would be this book. This book is something that is flowing into the family, whether because one family member is reading it and intends to pass along the information to other members or because someone who cares about the family is reading it to find out what can be done to help.

Each family has expectations of its members and of the family as a whole. When those expectations are not met, or when they change (as in the case of a suicide), the family is thrown out of balance. This is part of the challenge of keeping the family mobile in balance.

Family Traditions

Most families have traditions. Traditions are customs or practices that families have done for a period of time. With most families, they take place during holidays and/or other events like birthdays. Other families have certain events that they do year after year. However big or small, each family has them. They are unique to each family. Some family traditions might change after the loss, depending on who died in the family. However difficult this might be, the family has an opportunity to remember those good times while forging new traditions in the family.

These traditions also are important because they are part of the family system and how it communicates. We can examine the lives of our families and see what kinds of traditions we have. These can be small traditions, like eating a certain food on Christmas Eve, or large family gatherings on holidays. Whatever they are, they are important to the system because traditions, while they might change in the family unit, are significant in starting that new phase in the family after the death of one of its members.

The loss and the subsequent grief in the family system cause the family's development to be stunted or thrown off its natural course of progression. To use another metaphor, the fabric of the family has been torn and must be mended. A legacy of suicide has entered the family, if it was not already there. It is not unusual to start talking to survivors and find out that this is not the first suicide in the family. Many times, they will start thinking about it and realize that someone in a previous generation had killed him or herself. Or it could be that the legacy is much more intimate, as when a woman kills herself and then her daughter kills herself as well, believing she is destined for the same fate.

Promises are not always kept in families (for example, the promise to stay alive) and those broken promises linger in the lives of those who follow and also will alter the family's course. All these reactions will affect parenting and decisions made for the future.

Families can recover and move forward; however, it will take work to go in that direction, as well as to return balance to the mobile. But the family can still return to a functional state and find hope for the future. We must work hard to break the legacy of suicide in families, to rewrite history so that it does not include suicide in future generations.

7. Relationship Losses in the Family

Every family experiences relationship losses. Here we discuss the most common losses in the family and how suicide juggles them and spins them around.

Child Loss

A statistic floated around for years that 75 percent of marriages ended after the death of a child. No one ever was sure where it came from, leading The Compassionate Friends to conduct a telephone survey to check the reliability of the statistic (The Compassionate Friends, 2006). This research suggested that only 16 percent of marriages had ended after the death of a child, far from the 75 percent that had been accepted before. Most likely these marriages already were struggling before the child died and could not withstand the death of the child.

The parental relationship is strained after the suicide. Both the two people who are married have pasts that pre-date their married life. Each person comes into a marriage with his or her own set of baggage, experiences, culture, DNA, and everything else that makes up a human being. While they might or might not have experienced a loss before the loss of the child they created together, that loss tests the relationship.

Each parent will have expectations of how the other will grieve. A wife will assume that her husband will grieve just the way she does, and a husband will make the same assumption about his wife. They will be disappointed when that does not happen. They might even find themselves turning to the surviving children for support because they cannot come together and discuss the loss as parents. Or they might blame each other for what they feel their partner should or should not have done.

When a child dies, part of each parent dies in that child. They lose the goals and dreams they had for that child, no matter the age. All parents wish happiness for their children, and when a child dies, the parents may feel that they have failed the child, failed to keep him or her happy and in the world with us. Parents who lose younger children lose the opportunity to see that child married and have children. There are no grandchildren.

Parents who lose an adult child who was mentally ill may already have coped with the loss of dreams during the onset of the mental illness. They may even be partially relieved when an adult child dies, knowing they do not have to worry about the child for the rest of their lives, particularly as the parents grow older and might not be able to help and care for them.

Stepparents may feel a bit removed from the loss. They will want to support the spouse who is grieving the suicide of his or her child but a stepparent may not know how to do that. However, the stepparent who has raised the child with the biological parent has functioned as a full-time parent and may feel that he or she has lost a biological child.

The family that loses its only child becomes childless, just as it was before the child was born. Some parents may choose to have another child, sometimes called a replacement child, while others may be past that time in their lives where they want to raise another child and/or do not want the worry and fear that they had with the child who died. For the parents who choose to have another child, it is important to be aware that this child will not be a replica of the first child. It is an enormous burden for any child to have to live in the shadow of a sibling who died before he or she arrived.

What many parents who lose a child fail to see, however, is that their surviving children might be struggling. Often the parents are so engrossed in their grief that they cannot see beyond what they have lost. They forget about the surviving children who still need their parents to love and care for them.

Other parents worry incessantly about their surviving children. Sometimes they fear letting them out of their sight for fear of losing them, too. They worry when their children have a bad day (even their adult children). The thought of losing another child is unbearable.

Parents must keep the communication with one another open during this experience because it is often difficult for them know what the other is thinking. As parents might have surviving children to care for, plus jobs to continue, it might be difficult for them to seek grief support for themselves. Somehow they have to continue to guide and lead the family through this traumatic experience, and they need to come together to do that.

Parent Loss

When children, whether young, adolescent, or adult, lose a parent, it completely changes their world. The loss of a parent is the loss of a guardian and someone who forges the path to the future for the children. They are at least partially orphaned since one parent has died. And in suicide, they feel as if they have been abandoned because the person killed him or herself (there is no one and nothing to blame other than the parents themselves). Children are left without role models as they go forward into the future. They are left with one parent who must take on the roles of both mother and father even though they are not equipped to do so. Or they are left without their tie to who they are in the world.

The majority of parental suicides leave the children bewildered, no matter what age they are. They might fear that they too will die by suicide. If children are young, they will wonder if they caused the suicide to happen. Did they wish it on their mother or father because they were mad at them? Depending on their age, they might not understand what the parent was coping with (mental illness, alcohol abuse, work issues, and so forth). They might have thought the parent was the most important person in the world. And that person is gone.

When it comes time to marry and form their own families, sometimes children who have lost a parent to suicide choose not to have children (or decide not to name a child after the deceased parent) because they are afraid they are destining their children for suicide or at the very least putting them at risk for mental illness (Cain, 2006). This fear might seem unfounded to people looking in from the outside, especially if they see someone relating beautifully to other people's children. As a person bereaved by suicide, I can testify that the scars are deep where many outsiders cannot see them.

This is particularly true if the family did not discuss the suicide and the now adult child still has issues that resonate from unresolved grief relating to the loss. Although it is best to somehow resolve these with one's family, the passage of time sometimes makes such resolution impossible. The now-adult survivor should find some way to work through this issue.

Note that the elderly have a high suicide rate. A person who is sick and who has already lost his or her spouse may choose suicide because he or she believes it is time to move on, that his or her life on earth is finished, and there is no more reason to suffer. Members of families surviving that kind of suicide may not travel a typical suicide grief route because they understand why their parent chose suicide and they respect that decision.

Sibling Loss

The sibling relationship is complex, no matter where in the lifespan we are. In our childhoods, we typically spend more time with our siblings than anyone else; we teach each other how to communicate and function in the world; and we share more DNA and culture with them than anyone else. This does not mean it is an easy relationship, though. We argue with our siblings. Sometimes we physically fight them. We can be so much alike that we want to hurt each other, or we are jealous of each other. And when one dies, we react with a sense of heightened mortality because someone that close to us in age is not supposed to die young or leave us.

But it also is a relationship we take for granted.

Some of us who have lost a sibling to suicide never had the chance to grow up with them. We will spend the bulk of our lives carrying this loss with us. There are siblings who never knew each other because the older one died and then the younger one was a product of the parents' wanting to create another child. That sibling grows up in the shadow of someone he or she never met. These siblings know what happened to the sibling they have "replaced" and they wonder if they also will die by suicide at that age, or at any other time.

People often tell siblings to be strong for their parents. They do not mean to say this; they want to say something and simply do not know what else to say. They want to ease the pain in some way. What they do not realize is that the sibling might then wonder what his or her own grief is worth if he must put it aside for the parents. This question might set the sibling up for complicated grief.

Siblings are called the "forgotten mourners" or "double orphans" after they lose a sibling to suicide because not only have they lost a sibling, a playmate, someone with whom they shared a lot of memories, and someone who knew a lot about them, but they also have lost their parents for some time as the parents struggle to grasp the idea that they have lost one of their children. They also might have lost an ally to partner up against mom and dad or some other siblings. Perhaps the sibling who died was the one who protected the surviving sibling. Or the one who died was the one the surviving sibling protected. In either case, she surviving sibling might feel guilty for not keeping the brother or sister alive.

However, the siblings also might be relieved that the sibling died. It could have been that the family revolved around that sibling's mental illness. The family might not have had much structure because the parents were forced to constantly cope with unexpected episodes, outbursts, and/or brushes with the law. The surviving siblings have grown up in a home much like that with an alcoholic parent where what they think is normal probably is not for the majority of other families they know.

Even if they are children, siblings will feel the need to protect their parents. They see their parents hurting, possibly crying, and they do not want to see them hurt anymore. They realize that this hurt has changed the family. They choose not to tell their parents when bad things happen.

For many, the suicide will define their lives and choice of career. At school, if they were the younger sibling, they might feel stereotyped as "so and so's sibling." While this might have happened if the sibling were alive as well, now it has a different meaning since the sibling has died by suicide.

The sibling loss experience often shapes the romantic relationships these siblings will have. Some siblings will choose not to have children because they fear the experience of their parents. Or perhaps they feel as though they failed at keeping their sibling here on earth and do not believe they should have a child.

There are several types of sibling relationships, as I wrote about in my book for siblings after suicide (Linn-Gust, 2001). Even less than ten years after Denise's death, I saw how distinct the relationships were. One was what I call the parent-sibling relationship. That is where the sibling who dies is much younger than the surviving sibling. I always think of my sister Karen because she was ten years older than Denise and served as a surrogate mother to Denise when she was young. Much of Karen's grief reaction was similar to that of a parent losing a child.

Then there is the role model relationship where the sibling who dies is much younger than the sibling who survives. In that situation, the sibling who survives usually looked up to the older sibling as a role model even though there might have been parts of that sibling's life either that the surviving sibling never saw or that were hidden from him or her. When the older sibling dies, the sibling left behind is bereft of a role model. And that sibling might fear that he or she will die at the same age as the older sibling.

The friend-sibling relationship is the one I felt I shared with my sister Denise. We were less than four years apart, we shared a room for ten years, and growing up we did everything together. I see this relationship quite a bit on my web site in the guestbook, particularly for male-female sibling relationships. There are many females who are particularly saddened by their brothers' deaths because those brothers were integral to their world, their best friends. The loss leaves a huge void in their lives.

Finally, siblings who simply did not feel close to the one who died have a distant-sibling relationship. For several reasons, the surviving sibling may not appear to be grieving for the sibling who died. Perhaps the age distance between the two kept them from having much of a relationship (because the older sibling left home while the younger one was growing up) or because life in the family was very different (for financial or emotional reasons) when each one was growing up. Or it might be because the family unit as a whole was distant emotionally. This surviving sibling might not feel the need to grieve deeply for the deceased sibling. Instead the sibling might grieve for the relationship he or she realizes never existed.

The loss experience will be unique for each sibling in the family. While the siblings may share the same genes, they most likely will have been raised at different stages of the family's life, and the environment may have been different for each of them. Sometimes the siblings who survive a suicide may wonder how they are different from the sibling who died by suicide; the environment and experiences that each had will partly explain the difference.

Sometimes a sibling loses someone he or she detested (like a step sibling) because the family changed with a parent remarried. The surviving sibling in this case may feel guilty for such a reaction.

Twins have a unique relationship—about as close as two people can get without being the same person. But that does not mean they want to share everything. These two people, especially those who look alike, may have struggled in their lives to be separate, even to the point of alienating one another. In this case when one twin dies, the other realizes he or she may have missed out on something. If twins are very close, they can be each other's best friend because they can share everything. When one of such a pair dies, the survivor can feel a hole as well as a sense of survivor guilt, wondering why the other twin died and not him or her.

Half siblings do not always grow up together or know each other. They share one parent, but that doesn't mean they share the same lives. The parent they share might have had very different relationships with each of them, especially if there is a large age difference. But some half siblings are brought up together and are close in age. When one half sibling dies by suicide, the reaction to the suicide might depend on how much contact they had. If they were not very close (in several different ways), the surviving sibling might feel disconnected from the suicide, especially if he or she did not know the half sibling very well (or at all).

Step siblings do not always live together or they might be raised together, the same as half siblings. They, too, might feel disconnected from the sibling who died and/or the whole event since they are not biologically related and/or have little contact. They also might never have met the step sibling who died. Even though there will be a disconnect, the family dynamic will be affected by the suicide because the stepparent, the biological parent of the deceased, will be grieving.

In some families, there are people we call siblings who are not our parents' children. There are cultures that call cousins siblings. Or for some people, it might be best friends, people with whom they have been raised. For people who do not have any siblings (or do not get along with the siblings they do have), a best friend is someone they will say is "like a sister" or "is like a brother." While these relationships do not share the same biological connection as two siblings who are the product of the same two parents, they are relationships that need acknowledgment and should be respected when a person is grieving. And the bereaved person should not be afraid to say that he or she lost a brother or sister, because the relationship is unique. Returning to the beginning of this section, family is who we define it to be.

While usually included in extended family, siblings-in-law also should be included in this relationship category. For some surviving siblings, the in-law they lose could have been the only brother or sister they had. Suddenly, they too are siblingless and saddened that they have lost the brother or sister they had always wished for but did not get until they were adults.

Spouse /Partner Loss

Marriages are partnerships, and when one spouse dies, that leaves half of the membership alone. For the marriage that had no children, the remaining spouse might be left without a connection if the in-laws blame the spouse for the loss (or the spouse might blame the in-laws). When children are involved, the surviving spouse is left trying to raise a family and provide enough love and financial support to hold the family together while grieving the loss of one's life partner.

Sometimes the spouse kills himself and leaves behind a pregnant wife who must bear and raise a child alone, a child that she created with the deceased and had anticipated they would raise together. Spouses left behind with children also must play the roles of both parents and might not be comfortable with both roles. That spouse must be the decision maker, the disciplinarian, and do everything that was previously shared with the other spouse.

Or the parent will have to give up some of what he or she did in the family (like spending leisure time with the children) because food has to be put on the table. If a husband died and the mom is suddenly forced back to work, she will not have as much time for her children as she did before her husband died. The family's financial situation also might change and the family might have to move to a smaller house, rent an apartment, or possibly move in with grandparents. While it is not recommended that people make drastic changes until about a year after the death, sometimes these changes are inevitable because of finances. The surviving spouse will be struggling to keep the family together, the bills paid, and work through his or her grief.

Partner loss can be complicated if the couple was never married and, therefore, the family never recognized the partner. Without any legal say, the partner might not be able to retrieve the body, plan the funeral, or even have any access to benefits. Most important, the partner might be excluded from the support of the deceased's family and will have no one to recognize his or her grief. Suicide is complicated but this situation makes it more stigmatizing for the surviving person.

Typically part of spouse loss is the change in the social role for the surviving spouse after the death. Survivors often feel that society no longer considers them a parent, sibling, or other relationship to the person who died. For the spouse this feeling, even if not based in reality, can have broad implications. People are treated differently when they are single rather than part of a couple. Each person puts some aspect of themselves into the role, and when that role is lost, they must grieve for that loss as well (Silverman, 1988).

8. Other Family Relationships and Grief

Within a family, the roles and relationships, most of them biological, that we have to each other are affected after a loss by suicide. We have parents, siblings, children, pets, extended family, and the list goes on of the family members who are affected by the loss. In this chapter we discuss some of the relationships that often aren't acknowledged beyond the more immediate suicide losses of children, parents, siblings, and spouses.

Grandparents

When my sister died, my only living grandparents were my two grandmothers. My Grandma Linn was in a nursing home suffering from dementia. As far as I know, she was never told that Denise died because she was not living in present time (she often thought my dad was my grandfather). I remember going to visit my Grandma Zurawski in the months after Denise died. My mom had some photos of Denise and placed them on the kitchen table. Grandma kind of pushed them away and told my mom that it was too hard.

At the time, I was twenty-one, and I understood she was upset. We all were. Looking back, I can see where it saddened her because Denise was part of the family's future. No grandparent wants to see their adult children lose their children and hurt like that. Grandma died seven months after Denise so I never really had a chance to talk to her about Denise dying. And it was about fifteen years later before it occurred to me that she was a sibling survivor as well.

Often, as has been mentioned previously, there is another suicide somewhere in the family's history. In mine, it was my grandmother's brother. He died as an adult in the 1960s. He was a lawyer who had a second home on Lake Michigan. Beyond that, I do not know much about him and I remain sorry that I did not know enough at the time to ask Grandma Zurawski about her loss. It was different from mine, but it makes me wonder how Denise's death resonated in her mind, bringing back the emotions around her brother's death.

Grandparents hurt over the loss of their grandchildren because they want to see their offspring and the future generations prosper. Some grandparents have raised the person who died by suicide. They feel invested beyond the grandparent who only saw the person a few times a year. They might feel guilty and wonder what they did not do to help the person enough, or wonder if they missed something somewhere. These grandparents will have the same kinds of doubts and guilt that a parent might.

Grandparents may also feel a strong sense of the stigma and shame around suicide because they are older and remember when suicide was not talked about or people who died by suicide were not allowed burial in some cemeteries.

The Adopted

While many adopted people consider their adopted family their actual family, they still could be affected by a suicide loss in different ways than others. This is important to consider because it could alter their relationship with their adopted family. They could feel guilty that their being adopted into the family somehow caused the suicide. They also might fear, if a parent dies by suicide, that they will lose their place in the family.

Extended Family

Extended family can include aunts, uncles, cousins, and anyone else who might or might not have had regular contact with the person who died. Some aunts and uncles might have helped to raise the person. Cousins, as discussed in the sibling section, may feel as if they have lost a sibling.

Extended family members who lose someone they felt very close to will feel a sense of sadness that they missed something or they were not there enough for that person. They might wonder if they reached out one more time, would that have made a difference? And extended family members who did not have regular contact with the person who died will wonder why they did not reach out more often, realizing that time had passed and they missed out on spending time with that person. They also will wonder whether if they had taken the time for the person, they might have seen something that others missed.

Often, extended family members do not reach out for support after the suicide of a loved one. They do not believe they are included in the family. But this is irrelevant. Anyone who is affected by the loss should reach out. I often remind people that if you did not care about someone, you would not hurt.

Some extended family members might have been the people closest to the one who died. Someone could have lived with or been raised by an aunt and/or uncle. Their cousins might have been more like siblings to them. In this case, they are more than extended family, they are the immediate family and their loss should be acknowledged as such.

In-laws

In-laws may believe they are one step outside the family because they are not biological relatives. But even if they are parents-in-law watching their son-in-law grieve after his sibling dies, they will want to help and be supportive. Because they are one step outside the family, they actually might be better supports in some ways because they have less family history and might be able to offer compassion that does not include all the immediate family complexities. They just want to help.

Friends

It is even more difficult for friends to find support after a suicide. When one is not married into a family or biologically related, people usually will wonder why the person is so upset. There are several types of friends who will be affected by a suicide.

One friend might be a very close friend of the person who died. This person might have felt that the one who died was like a sibling (as discussed in the sibling section). They feel many of the emotions that siblings do after the suicide. And they might not feel included in all the family events because they are not biological relatives. There are families who do a good job of including friends in the rituals following a suicide. However, as time goes on, the friends might not believe they should be contacting the family and may shy away. I know of other friends who still remain in contact with the family of the deceased loved one, even many years later. Or the family might not have known that the two people were friends (particularly if there was a relationship that the deceased was afraid to share with the family—like a gay relationship that was instead portrayed as a close friendship). Without contact from the friend, the family will not know to reach out to that person.

My personal experience is that families want to hear from the friends. We wanted to hear from Denise's friends because they had stories to tell about her that we did not know. The world becomes a little smaller when a loved one dies and, because there will be no new memories, it is great when more people share the ones that they have.

The friends, though, may be afraid to reach out because they feel awkward. They may believe they are not really part of the family (especially if the family did not know about them) or they might be embarrassed that they feel that sad about a friend dying since society places the emphasis of loss on the immediate family.

Some friends feel guilty because they were not available for the friend who died. And they feel guilty for the circumstances that surrounded why they were not available. It might have been that their own lives were busy or they felt consumed with their own problems. But if the person who died had a difficult marriage and home life, the friend may not have felt welcome around the spouse and chose to stay away. What they didn't know was that their friend, though unable to welcome their support, could have used it.

Sometimes friends of the one who died stay away because they know something about the suicide. I mentioned in the grief chapter that Denise had a suicide pact with at least one other girl. That girl had made prior attempts, and when someone found out she was planning to kill herself she was put on a watch. However, she never mentioned Denise's intent to die. That girl obviously has to live the rest of her life with this knowledge. She told me about a year after Denise died. One other friend, who I mentioned earlier has been silent, probably also knows something but has chosen not to speak to us since shortly after the funeral. The reason they do not come around is about them, not us. But it is hard for us to see that, particularly when we are entrenched in our raw grief.

Other friends who are affected include the friends of the loved ones in the family, but not necessarily the friends of the one who died. These people will want to help a hurting friend as much as possible. Unless they knew the deceased really well, they probably will not consider themselves bereaved by the suicide. Instead, I see these people as wanting to help the person they care about. These are the people (often neighbors fall into this group) who will show up with the casseroles or volunteer to answer the phone. They want to do something, and they are able to help out with some of the tasks the family might forget to do or not want to do.

These friends also might not know the whole story about the person who died and in time will make good listeners. Because they want to help, it is an opportunity to forge a new relationship with them and let them learn more about their friend. While they might not have been family to the person who died, they are family to a loved one of the one who died.

Pets

A change in the family sometimes leads to the more intimate inclusion of a pet as a family member. Since Hurricane Katrina, when people refused to evacuate their homes because their pets were not allowed to go to the shelters (and the people had nowhere else to go), there has been more acknowledgment that pets are members of families and should be allowed to evacuate with a family rather than be left behind.

When a death occurs in a family, the pet is acutely aware of what has happened. I still can remember arriving at my parents' house after my sister died. The house was filled with people, mostly family, and there was Chaos, the family German Shepherd, in the midst of it all. My older sister Karen remembers that Chaos ran out to greet me when I drove up. What I remember was Chaos looking confused in the midst of all of us crying and laughing (probably at the same time). And in the days to come, Chaos would look for Denise each day at the time when she was supposed to be getting home from school.

Although we do not truly know what a pet gets from a family because they cannot speak to us, we do know that they can be affected by the death of a loved one. For some pets, the person who died was the caretaker, perhaps the person who fed and walked the dog or slept with the cat. When that person is gone, the pet will sense the absence. People have reported that their dogs go looking for the deceased loved ones.

Pets will be confused about what is ensuing in the family house. They will not understand why people are upset, why they are coming and going. Nor will they understand why people might be stopping by. But in this time, they can serve as supports for family members. They will be missing the loved one who died (especially if that person was the caretaker of the pet), but they will be there for the surviving family members. Just like children, they want their routine to resume. For dogs, they look to their pack for leadership.

For some people, the pet will be the last connection to a family member. Obviously, this makes the pet very important in the bereaved person's life. There are families who might take in the pet of a loved one who had nowhere else to go because that person lived alone. In those families, the pet will be a connection to the loved one.

If a person does end his or her life, a pet may be thrust upon a family member who is not prepared. While I understand that it is difficult when a dog or a cat (or multiples of each) is at the doorstep looking for a new home, a hasty decision should not be made if the family is not comfortable taking the animal in. A pet needs as much love and care as possible because the pet has lost its home and may be living with people it does not know. The pet will return that love and care (this will be discussed in a later chapter).

While there is no data to support this statement, I have heard anecdotally from suicide attempters and clinicians that pets sometimes are the reasons that people do not end their lives. Pets provide something in their lives that maybe they do not believe they get from humans and may give them something to take care of, a reason to get up each morning and face the day.

When the pet who survives the dead person comes to the end of its life (as they do not live as long as most humans), it can seem like a repetition of the loss of the loved one. But remember that the animal we take in under these circumstances provides the family with more years of love. It is important that after loss we remember not to shut anyone or anything out despite our pain for the person we have lost.

These are not the only family relationships affected after the suicide loss of a loved one. I am sure there are many more that I did not include because, again, each family defines itself uniquely. If you are in one of those relationships, do not be afraid to tell people how the loss has affected you. Often, people react in strange (to put it kindly) ways because it is new to them. By trying to understand their perspective and letting them know about something of which they were previously unaware, you are giving them an education that they will thank you for later.

9. The Lifespan and Grief

People cope differently with grief at different points in their lives. One of the most challenging aspects of grief in a family is that each family member will be in a different place. In addition to being different just because we are, family members also will be at different stages of the lifespan and therefore in different developmental stages.

A note about helping children, adolescents, and teens through grief. Because they are school age, it is be imperative to involve the school community just because of the amount of time a child or teen spends at school each day. There is no such thing as too much support for these groups of young people because they will feel the effects of suicide ripple through their entire lives. By helping them early and continually as they grow and develop, we will give them a chance of leading happier, healthier lives.

The resources section at the end of the book also offers more information on how to talk to children about suicide and suggests keepsake journals for teens to fill out to remember a loved one. There also are lists of books for children, adolescents, and teens about coping with loss, although several are not specific to suicide loss (and are noted as so).

Children

People often don't think babies and children not yet in school are grieving. However, on some level they are aware that something is happening. And they will know that someone is missing. Be open with them about what is happening (if they are talking and understand language). There is more information below on how to talk to children about suicide. While there are developmental stages that all children travel through, they travel through them at different times. Therefore, some children might be ready for more information than other children of the same age. As the parent, you know your children best.

Children do not need to know all the details at once. It is okay to tell them that their loved one died and explain that they had a brain disease. It is important to say that it was not because they did not love the child, but that they were in a lot of pain and could not feel beyond that. Children will take the information and use it to conjure something that makes sense to them.

A good example of this comes from Joanne Harpel, the Director of Survivor Initiatives for the American Foundation for Suicide Prevention. When Joanne's brother killed himself, her son was three years old. She told her son that his uncle "had an illness in his brain" and that was what caused him to die by suicide. However, her son could not recall the word *illness* and instead used the word *enormous* as in "tell me again about the enormous that made Uncle Stephen die." *Enormous* captures everything about suicide loss. And it is a good reminder to listen to children. Sometimes they can explain suicide and loss better than adults.

Children do not need to be overloaded with information. If they have questions, they will ask. As they grow older, they will have more questions. The key is to let them know that it is okay to ask. And as their understanding develops, they comprehend more. Much of what they will want to know is usually about the person who died. They will want to know about their personalities and what they were like. Sometimes explaining to them right away that it was a suicide can prevent their feeling the stigma later on, by which time they will have long since separated how the person died from who they were in life. This will not be the case for all children, but the openness about the death that they can sense from the beginning can make all the difference in the world for them as they grow up.

Grieving in front of children is good. Often, parents are afraid to break down because they do not want their children to see them upset or sad. When children see their parents feeling sad for their loved one, they know that it is okay for them to grieve, too. Their grief will be somewhat different, though. They will grieve as much as they can at one time and then might go off and play for a while as if nothing has happened. Developmentally, they know what they can handle and they will return to it when they are ready.

At some point school-age children are sent back to the classroom. In the years after I was a high school teacher, I had a discussion with one of the counselors at the school where I taught. She explained that after a funeral a student is brought into the counseling office, asked if s/he is okay, told they have help if they need it, and sent back to class. She acknowledged it is not a great way to help a grieving student. Keep in contact with the school about how the child is doing even months and years after the suicide.

What children need most is to know their security is still there. And they find their security in their routine. While it might be difficult for a family to return to a routine, especially if a parent has died, children need to know that they will go back to school, that they will get dinner in the evening, and that someone will be there to put them to bed. What children want and need seems simple but often the simple and routine parts of life are overlooked, particularly when a suicide has uprooted the world as the family once knew it.

If the children do not get their routine back, they may try to re-create it by taking care of their parents. Because the parent is incapacitated with the emotions of suicide grief, the child might take on the role of the parent, doing tasks that the child is not developmentally ready for. It is not unheard of that children are doing the chores, making dinner, and getting a parent off to work after a loss. The parent also might come to the child wanting the child to reassure him or her that everything will be okay. Children (and teens) do this because they want life to get back to normal and the only way they can see this happening is by their taking on these roles.

Children and adolescents may fear reaching the age of the loved one who died. And for children who have lost a sibling, that might not be very far away. I have had people tell me that for years they never thought they would live beyond the age of a parent who died. When they did reach that age, they felt a little strange about it, but after it passed, they realized the fear was irrational. It might have been irrational but probably no one sought to help them understand that one person's time of death will not be the same for another and the fear instead festered in their minds.

Younger family members can be more affected by the loss than older family members (even teens who are off with their friends or involved with school activities and not home very often). The more time spent at home, especially with the person who died, the more likely they might need some extra help with their grief.

More support groups for all age groups (children through young adult) are forming around the world, which helps them feel less isolated. For years, people thought that children did not grieve and would not be affected by loss. But what people did not understand is that young people have to carry the death with them for a long way through their lives. They need help integrating it early and giving it a place so that they can have long, happy lives ahead of them filled with hope.

Adolescents/Teens

Young people in the adolescent and teen years are looking to separate themselves from their families. They are carving out their identities. They want to be independent, individual people. When someone they care about dies by suicide, they might find themselves wanting to retreat back to their families but afraid to do so. In a time when they want be separated from their families, they inversely want to be intertwined with their friends and peers. Having a suicide in the family makes them feel like they stick out like a sore thumb.

They need to know their family members are there to listen and support them. They also need to know of any trusted relatives, school personnel, and other adults who are there for them as well. Whoever is important in their lives will need to be open with them and ready to listen. Their friends also will be key for providing support and helping them to feel normal by continuing to spend time with them. Parents of friends will need to educate their children on how to help the grieving friend.

Adolescents and teens who are involved in various activities may cling to the activities to help them feel normal. Looking forward to practice and being part of that ritual daily after school might be what keeps them motivated. Time should be spent helping their teammates or friends involved in the activity to understand what the bereaved teen is coping with so that they can understand how best to help that person. The teen might be looking for this particular group of people to be the sounding board if s/he believes she cannot talk about it at home.

In 2010, as I write this, how we grieve has changed thanks to the advent of social networking media. Not just for adolescents, Facebook and My Space pages, where loved ones and friends can remember the person who died, provide comfort because people reach out and share their memories and what the person who died meant to them. Parents should monitor this activity as it will give insight to the teen's feelings that he or she might not be sharing otherwise.

We also have to be in tune with adolescents to make sure that this experience will not make them think suicide is the answer or that it is a way to get attention in society. Typically, prior to this loss (unless they have had a prior loss), their only experience with suicide will be via television and film. There is a teaching opportunity not to be lost to educate adolescents at this time on the warning signs of suicide and where to turn for support. And this includes the reminder to them to reach out for help themselves if they feel overwhelmed by life.

College Students

When a college student loses a loved one to suicide, often the student is away from home. He or she might come home for a few days (as I did) but feel he or she must return to campus and get back to school. That is what I felt. Some students will not go back, sometimes because the family's financial picture has changed or because other family members do not want them to be away from the family. My mom told me later that she did not want me to go but knew she could not stop me. I just wanted some sort of a routine because in my life that always has been what has sustained me through unpredictable emotions and times.

It is also difficult for college students because at that time in life, not many people have experienced losses in their lives. College students traditionally have a hard time finding people to relate to. They are away from home (and thus away from the main support system of the family) and with a group of people who might shy away from the person because they have not experienced any death in their own lives.

Although this is changing, college campuses also have lacked support for students. It was as if college-age students dropped off the radar mental health–wise while they were away at school. Campus counseling was minimal at best, but that is changing. Today parents who have students in college should easily be able to find out what kind of services campuses offer for their grieving children.

While we often speak of adolescence as a difficult time, people forget that college can be just as difficult. Students are at least somewhat on their own (maybe not paying the bills but making decisions about what to eat for dinner, when to do the laundry, and all the other items that their parents might have at least helped with prior to moving to a campus community). They are trying to decide what they will do with their lives after graduation, what kind of career they will have, and how they will support themselves.

Grief thrown on top of that is a one-two punch. Suddenly, a student is not only trying to figure out who he or she wants to be, but is also digesting a major loss in his or her life, one that forces re-evaluation of all values and goals.

In many ways, it is easier for people to keep in touch now with cell phones, texting, and the Internet. These are some ways for parents to keep in contact with their grieving children, if only to get a grief-journey temperature check. College students also need to understand that their parents might need to hear from them periodically to know that they are okay. Because the parents also are devastated by the loss, they might fear losing the student as well, and the student may be equally fearful of another loss.

I spent the summer after my sister's death as a communications intern at USA Boxing at the U.S. Olympic Training Center in Colorado Springs, Colorado. Sponsored by a major national phone carrier, in the lobby where everyone checked into the center was what we dubbed "the five-minute phone." We could call anyone anywhere in the United States, but we could only talk for five minutes. Sometimes there would be a line of people waiting. But if you hit it just right, there was not a line and you could talk longer. I would sneak in there when I could and call my parents or my older sister or some of my friends. Long distance was still on calling cards in the early 1990s and we only had a pay phone in our dorm building. While that might seem primitive, it is a reminder of how easy staying connected is today.

Young Adulthood

It is not really fair to lump all of adulthood in the one section. After all, what a person experiences at thirty is very different from the grief experience of sixty.

For young adults, some of their experience with loss will mirror that of a college student. While college students are still separating themselves from their families, often by living away from home for school, young adults might have moved back in with their parents following college to save money (or might never have left!). The world is often still one's oyster at this time. While some people might marry early, people are marrying later than in the past, giving young adults more freedom to experience life and its opportunities. When they experience a loss at this time of their lives, it leaves them with a sense that the world is not their oyster. But it can also make a young adult realize early that it is most important to pursue what one really wants from life and make life that much more fulfilling.

Middle Adulthood

Adults who are in the midst of life when they experience a loss typically are in situations where they cannot make changes (or it would be very difficult to make changes) since they are supporting a family. They have a lifestyle they enjoy and also might be afraid to leave a job. People often are more settled, although maybe not happily, in middle adulthood. The loss of the loved one to suicide throws anything settled out the window and the person then must decide if it is worth the life change to pursue a dream or something he or she has been contemplating for some time.

Late Adulthood

For people in late adulthood, also known as the elderly, they might not feel a need to grieve deeply for the person who died because (if they believe in an afterlife) they believe they will see them soon. But for some bereaved, particularly those who have lost a spouse with whom they had a long relationship, they might lose all interest in their lives and contemplate suicide themselves. It is important to check on the elderly who are grieving and keep them connected, especially if the person who died was their last surviving family member or the last person of their generation.

Gender and Grief

Gender differences play a part in grief. The majority of people who attend support groups are women. We often joke that women like to talk, talk, talk. But when we started a second support group in Albuquerque, about half the attendees were men. One day we split by gender and could not get the men to come back to the mixed-gender group. I had someone ask me later if we served them steak to lure them in. However, the reality is that it is just not about men and women. As I'll explain below, we use gender as a way to label people because of how gender roles are conditioned in our society.

I attended a suicide survivor healing conference in Norway in 2005 and heard a psychologist, Oddbjorn Sandvik, discuss gender differences. He said that women often serve as "the grief boss," taking the initiative in grief and leading the way with language. Men then become preoccupied, worried about saying the right thing because they want to follow the wife's lead.

However, men also have a tendency to hang their grief on a hook and take it down from time to time when they choose to. Often they do not need to say as much in as many words as women might. Many times men will leave a conversation and women will think the men lack feelings, but they might come back to the conversation later because they had too many feelings and felt they could not share.

These misinterpretations freeze couples in their roles, and they stop communicating. Couples need to see these differences to inspire each other rather than allowing their roles to divide them.

Kenneth Doka and Terry Martin took these ideas one step further in their book, *Men Don't Cry . . . Women Do: Transcending Gender Stereotypes of Grief.* They used personality types rather than gender to describe grief because sometimes people of the opposite sex fall into a category unexpected for their gender. Intuitive grief, usually associated with women, is mostly about expression and exploration of feelings, while instrumental grief is mostly behavioral, revolving around thinking and doing. For example, intuitive grievers more likely would be found at a support group where they could express their feelings while instrumental grievers more likely would be found trying through advocacy to save others from dying by suicide. Some people might combine the two styles.

The reality is that most of us never use personality types to describe grief because we continue to condition and stereotype people by gender. Disentangling gender from grief is no different than seeing that grief is an individual journey. As the man who spoke at the conference in Norway said, we need to find a balance between women (grieving) and men (the reconstruction of one's life). Grief fills a gap between the past and the future. It is a journey that takes us from one point to the next, letting us process our emotions and understand how our lives have changed.

10. The Family Unit's Grief Reaction

Once we take into account the many things that happen to us individually during grief, then we can step back and acknowledge what happens to the family. Looking at the family as a system, or a group, is important because the actions and reactions of each person affect the others—including the action of the person who died by suicide.

Yet why is it that some families are able to cope better than others after a loss, particularly a suicide? Why can some families experience a loss but seemingly move forward and "be okay" while others cannot quite function productively again? And why can some families move forward more quickly than others?

There are multiple answers to these questions. What affects a family as a unit is closely aligned with how a person copes after the loss of a loved one. Some of what affects how the family will cope was explained in a previous chapter on relationships, but here we will discuss more issues that might influence how the grief experience pans out.

Previous losses and how the family coped with them are one determinant for how a family will function. Families need to know their histories and how they have reacted to changes in the past. Change is difficult and loss brings a lot of change with it.

Suicide is not part of the normal course of family development. If it were, we would be better prepared to cope with it. A suicide will alter the family in ways that many people probably cannot predict.

Perceptions of the deceased loved one change after any death but in one complicated like suicide, they provide very different perspectives. Some family members might only remember the bad times with the person who died and be grateful they are gone. Other family members might feel sadness for the same reasons, sad that the person never took the chance on life he or she wanted them to have. Or some people may only remember the good. A child or teen in the home may remember the sibling being shuttled from hospital to hospital, yet all Mom and

Dad can talk about is how wonderful the sibling was. It is important that people spend time working through some of the more difficult/sad memories because that can help them to deal with the definition of the death as a suicide. Once that process has been completed, the person can separate the life he or she shared with the loved one from how the loved one died.

When the deceased suffered from a mental disorder, the family might have revolved around that person and his or her problems. The family might have felt stigmatized for years and then even more shamed after the suicide, believing that people were saying that suicide was inevitable for the mentally ill person. It might not have been a mental disorder that someone suffered from; he or she may simply not have experienced the quality of life they wanted. Or the person did not want to burden the family anymore. The family might have feared that the person would die by suicide because of the pain they felt from the illness. The family might have already suffered a loss with the deceased when the illness was diagnosed. For parents who have children who suffer from any disability, at diagnosis they realize their children will never have the lives they hoped for when they brought them into the world. They suffered one loss with the child's illness, and the suicide is another.

Earlier, we discussed the uniqueness of the suicide grief experience, how some of it is related to the death being self-inflicted but also, like an accident, unanticipated. A high level of trauma can accompany the suicide grief experience when the death is a shock or a surprise. But as the previous paragraph points out, suicide is not always unanticipated. More likely, that anticipation is not acknowledged in families. And this reality can cause further division in families as some members will wonder why they were not asked to help the person who died.

Loved ones can live in fear of the possible suicide of someone they care about. After an attempt, or during the ideation (when someone is thinking about suicide), family members often are removing possible methods a person might use to kill him or herself and keeping a vigilant eye out for the loved one's behavior. But deep inside them, they know that they cannot control all that a loved one chooses to do. For these families, when a suicide happens, they knew that it was not a matter of if but rather when the person would die (Maple et al., 2007).

When the loved one has died by suicide but also killed people before turning a method on himself (called homicide-suicide), family members will find themselves in a quandary for support. Often, the people who lost loved ones through the murder will not feel sympathetic to the suicide survivors, believing that their loved one deserved to die because he or she took another life (or lives) away.

When homicide-suicide happens, a father might kill his wife and then kill himself, possibly leaving a group of children without parents. The children may then be shuttled off to grandparents who might have a different view of suicide, one stuck in the heightened stigma of society of generations past.

Suicide can be the ultimate betrayal in a family. Family members think they have open and honest relationships with each other, and when the person dies, they feel as if that trust has been violated.

Some family members do not have an opportunity to say goodbye to the loved one. This can happen for a variety of reasons. There are family members who cannot return for the funeral or memorial. While these often are difficult times for families, they also can be times where families come together and are able to talk through the loved ones' lives and what led to the suicide. Family members who cannot attend the mourning rituals should find a way to cope with the details, perhaps by contacting loved ones and talking through the loss with them. However, there also are loved ones who are denied the opportunity to say goodbye. This could be because the family member is not told about the death. Perhaps the family was estranged from this person in some way. If this happens, the family member who has been kept from the funeral needs additional outlets to cope with the loss. This could be through other family members and/or friends. Finally, children and teens sometimes are not allowed the opportunity to attend a funeral and/or memorial. They always should be given the choice to go. If they choose not to, it is okay, but the choice should be theirs. No matter what happens, family members all should have an opportunity to say goodbye to the loved one. This is only one step on the journey, but saying goodbye allows us to move forward with grief.

There is one theory that gives a good description of what happens in a family after a loss and describes a family after a suicide loss, too. The Integrated Individual-Family Model (Moos, 1995) discusses both the individual and family unit pieces of grief.

- Changes in who talks to whom and in what way

After a suicide, everything changes; there is no doubt about that. There is a sense of "no holds barred" in families after suicide as well. If there was anger, or anything else lingering below the surface, this is when it comes out, typically with a vengeance. But it can also mean that family members who have not have relied on each other before find they need one another for emotional survival.

People find out a lot about their families after a suicide. Sometimes they find out what they did not know was going on with their loved one. They realize that some members of the family knew all the details while others did not. The older the person who died, the more people are involved (as people marry, etc.), and the situation can become more complicated.

• Reconnection or cutoff of certain family members

Some family members will be angry at others for not being around (physically and/or emotionally) for the one who died. They might blame one person for the death and cut that person out of the family. If the suicide scares a family member, that person may cut him or herself out of the family, maybe not physically but emotionally (or both). Such a withdrawal may happen because the one family member that the person felt closest to is the one who died, or simply because the person can't handle the suicide itself and how it has changed the family.

It is possible that some family members will reconnect after the loss, that they will take this time to come back together after they have been emotionally apart for a long time. They will realize that they have lost one member and do not want to lose any others, or recognize how precious time is and that anyone could die on any day. This mostly appears to happen when aunts and uncles reconnect, or even connect for the first time, with the nieces and nephews of the sibling who died. They know they have the opportunity to keep their sibling alive for the children through the memories and do not want to miss that.

• Confusion in family roles (who is in charge and who has what responsibilities)

Children are particularly affected by this kind of confusion. Often their parents are too devastated by the loss of a child or a spouse to remember the rest of the family. No one forgets their surviving children on purpose; they just cannot see beyond the hole that the death has punched in their lives. Children crave routine, normalcy. If Mom and Dad are not cooking dinner, the children might try to do it themselves. If the house is a mess, they might try to clean it. They might make decisions for the family and take on roles they are not developmentally ready for.

Parents also might fear disciplining a child because they do not want to upset the child. Grief makes us do things we would never have expected to do; we never can predict how it will make us act. By not disciplining children. parents may reinforce troublesome behavior, when the misbehaving children are simply looking for someone to acknowledge that they are there and that there is some normalcy, although it will never be the same as it was before the loved one died.

- Overprotecting each other

This happens in several situations. While some parents might not discipline their children, others will be afraid to let them out of their sight because they do not want anything to happen to them. Children who know more about what happened to a sibling (through their relationship or through school) might not share with their parents details that they fear will hurt the parents. They do not want their parents to hurt more than they already are.

Parents who know details might not share them with their children, or even their spouse. This is done not to hurt them but to keep them from being hurt more. Parents, for example, sometimes change the story about how the person died. They do not want anyone hurt.

Sometimes one person might be the only one to know it is a suicide while all the other family members are led to believe it was something else (like an accident). While this ultimately hurts the family members who are not told (because they usually will learn the family secret eventually), it also hinders the grief process of the person who knows it was a suicide because that person cannot share it with anyone else.

Even though suicides are not covered up as they once were (although it still happens; often the coroner or medical examiner will rule in any way possible to avoid the suicide ruling which is why many one-car crashes are ruled accidents when they really might have been suicides), people sometimes do change the story despite what is typed on the death certificate. This too is not done in malice or to hurt anyone; people erroneously believe that by covering it up, they are saving themselves and the family members a lot of grief and difficulty coping. What they do not realize is that it actually has just the opposite effect. I know of one woman who was told, in her teen years, that her mother died of cancer. She found out in her thirties that it actually was a suicide. Suddenly, she had to re-grieve her mother's death all over again, this time as a suicide. I am sure that the family members only wanted to protect her, never realizing they would ultimately cause her more pain.

Young children who are in school sometimes know a death was a suicide but their family members have not told the school. Yet everyone knows it was a suicide. The child goes off to school and everyone knows it is a suicide but no one wants to say anything to the child, thinking the child does not know it is a suicide. It is also possible that the child has not been told it's a suicide, yet everyone else does know that (and sometimes the child knows even though everyone else does not realize it). The more changed stories are told, the more complicated things become.

Overprotecting also happens in support groups, particularly when adult children come with their parents. They might sit next to their mother and when each person in the group says who they lost and a little bit about their story, the adult children might not speak or might say very little. Sometimes they know something about the person who died, or the suicide, but do not want to share it because they do not want the parents to hurt more than they already are.

- Family becoming isolated from friends and support network

I felt as if we were living in a bubble when Denise died. Sometimes we seemed to be looking out of the bubble at everyone asking, "Why won't you all talk to us?" and everyone else was looking in saying, "We do not know what to say." That bubble was the house we lived in, and everyone else was gathered outside looking at us, many too upset to speak, and others too afraid to speak.

The systems perspective is important here. The family system feels separated from the outside environmental system (the community which is known as the suprasystem). Suicide can act as a wedge that comes between the family and the friends and support network. The issues surrounding suicide in general (like the shame and stigma) coupled with the family's embarrassment that it happened to them cause the isolation. There are times, too, when a family will isolate itself, not even realizing what it is doing. This is a coping mechanism, even if not an effective one, and might be the only one that the family (or members of the family) knows.

Suicide often involves mental illness, sometimes manifested in drug and alcohol abuse. For many years, the family might have hidden behind closed doors, not wanting anyone to see what really was going on in the house. I have heard stories of people who dressed family members to make them appear to be at least half functioning when people came over. Other families have hidden their loved ones, afraid of embarrassment by their actions.

These families can be described as closed systems. Their fear is what keeps them from reaching out. They do not want anyone to know what is really happening. When there is a suicide, they might try to cover it up, not wanting to add to the stigma already attached to the family because of one family member. They might fear opening the system lest everyone find out that the appearances are not what they seem.

Other families feel relief from the death and, while they may have to cope with their guilt, they also may finally open the curtains in the house, letting everyone see what happened now that there is no reason to cover it up. These families will be the most receptive to help but will need time to unravel the issues in which they have been wrapped up for years.

- Some families might have more than one mentally ill family member, and that other family member will need more support following the suicide.

Relationships to the person who died will affect how a suicide is grieved. Was everyone getting along well when the person died? If the person who died was not functioning well, there may have been ongoing or unresolved arguments. Such festering wounds can leave the loved ones with extra guilt that the last conversation had been angry. Some people might not have been physically and/or emotionally present in the relationship either because of business in their own lives (this is particularly true for adult siblings who have families of their own beyond their birth family) or a strained relationship with the one who died.

If the relationship was strained, it will make the grief process more difficult. There will be more roads to travel to process the relationship and learn how to let go what cannot be changed because of the words said (or the words that were not said).

Even if a relationship was fairly good before the suicide, grieving a suicide death is not simple because everyone has to cope with his or her own issues that may or may not even relate to the person who died. Issues that might not relate to the death include abandonment or fear of being alone. When a loved one dies, those fears come through and need to be coped with separately from the death.

For instance, a wife whose husband kills himself might have abandonment issues that go back to her relationship with her parents although they have nothing to do with her husband (yet they might have caused some tension in her relationship with her spouse). When her husband killed himself, she felt abandoned by him although his suicide might have had nothing to do with her (and everything to do with fears about his own life and failures). She will have to cope with these issues as well as grieve the fact that he died by suicide.

What else is going on in a person's and a family's life when there is a suicide? Is it a difficult time because of job loss, marital difficulties, school exams, moving, or any other potentially stressful event(s)? The reality is that life is never devoid of stress, particularly stress that causes tension, depression, and sleeplessness. As I age, I believe that half of what life is about is coping with stress (and the other half is about learning to communicate with people). When someone dies by suicide, we have to add another level of stress to our plates as we try to comprehend the loss of a loved one by suicide. For some people, this can be a breaking point, so finding extra support at this time (or alleviating some stress by eliminating situations that are causing stress, if possible) is crucial.

But there also could be good things going on in one's life at this time. A woman could be planning her wedding when her father kills himself. She had planned for him to walk her down the aisle, and now he will not be there to do that for her. She might be devastated by this, and even believe he purposely hurt her by missing her wedding although his suicide had nothing to do with her. She will have to find resolution for her wedding. It will not be the same but maybe her brother will walk her down the aisle and maybe a candle can be lit for her father in recognition that while he is not there, he is still part of her family and her important day.

Are there other losses in a family's history? Some families do not have a long history together. They might be very young families (maybe only two people who have just married) or blended families that are created when two parents come together with several children. In some families, one side might have experience with loss and the other might not. There might not be any past loss, or this death might be one of several. Whatever the family's history is, it is important to consider earlier losses because they will help determine how the family will react to the suicide.

It is also important to look at not only how the family coped with past losses, but also how the family copes with stress. Does the family have coping skills that are productive? The family may be able to find help more easily if they can identify what they have been through previously. I realize this is easy for me to say but not so easy to accomplish. Usually there is one family member who is aware of this kind of information because that person has processed it and thought about it before. It is not always one of the parents; it could be one of the children (although more likely an adult child than an adolescent).

While any type of past loss will help determine the family's reaction to the suicide, so will knowing if there are suicides in the family's history. As discussed earlier, there is a genetic component to suicide, and when suicide becomes part of one's vocabulary in what I call "a close and personal way," there is the reality that if it happened once, it could happen again.

I have had many conversations with the bereaved in the course of which they look at me and say, "You know, I didn't think about it, but my great uncle [or some other relative] killed himself." When someone dies by suicide, we start looking at our family trees and can see someone else in the past who died by suicide. We might not even have known that person or known much about them until a suicide in the family affects us in that close and personal way, and then we begin to search out the details. As we often say, we have to break the legacy of suicide in families.

When there is a suicide in a family, not all members are going to tell the same story around it. Remember that game "telephone" that starts out with one person whispering one sentence to the next person? By the time the sentence gets whispered to the person at the end of the line, it is totally different. We all see, hear, and understand things differently. Our perspectives are different, and that is why we can't walk in each other's shoes.

If you lined up a bereaved family and asked each of them to say what they believed happened to the deceased family member, my guess is that they would each tell you something slightly different. Each one had a different relationship with the loved one who died, and our perspectives are unique to each of us. We must honor and respect that in each of our family members.

Elderly people have a higher rate of suicide than many other age groups. A grandmother could die of natural causes and the grandfather, not wanting to be alone, might follow with a suicide, wanting to rejoin his loved one. The family left behind has suddenly lost both its matriarch and patriarch at one time and must digest two significant losses in a short period of time. Or an aging parent who is dying of a terminal illness might arrange his or her death so he or she does not have to endure a long, painful death. This can be difficult for some family members to accept even though the grandparent is at peace with it, a combination that causes friction when some family members accept this choice while others do not.

Because of financial difficulties, families are sometimes forced to move in with relatives, and those relatives might have different views about suicide.

Maybe they never liked the person the surviving partner was married to and will let the spouse and children know now that the person has died. If a spouse dies, the surviving spouse might eventually remarry, once again causing change, particularly for the children.

Cracks in families run deeper after suicide. The cracks need tending, whether by filling them with concrete or encouraging them to grow flowers. Everything that was going on should be explored as that will help the family understand where it needs to start to heal.

Because loss tests everything about us—our values, our patience, our relationships—we probably learn more about our family members, good or bad, during this time than at any other time in our lives. The crucial part is how we process what we learn and use it to make our families strong again.

FINDING HOPE

11. Directions

Each family and each individual travels its own road, so remember, as you read this chapter, that not everything suggested below will work for your family and/or all its members. Take what you need and leave the rest. Or revisit it later; you might find something new that you did not see before, or something that might not have worked for you or your family at that time might work now.

While some of the information is geared toward individuals, some of it also is focused on the family as a unit. The point of putting it all in one chapter is that some of it might be good to pass along to other family members and also might serve as discussion points to help family members process their grief together.

The ideas I offer come from my own grief experience and the experiences of people worldwide who have shared their stories with me. My goal is to try to give each family as many options as possible. But some people might go to a support group and realize they are not comfortable there. Or they might read a recommended book and find that it does not work. Do not give up. When you find what works, you will know. There is something along the road just for you.

One of the major pieces of coping with a traumatic loss is the need to tell the story repeatedly. While this isn't true for everyone (think back to the part about gender, grief, and personality types), for quite a few bereaved, the telling of the story is key to coping. Later in this chapter we discuss attending support groups, but a group setting is not necessarily for everyone (or available). Some people find good support from friends and other communities. They also chose other methods of self expression (such as some form of art).

Telling the story is a process rather than an event (Cain, 2002). During the telling of the story, the teller will reshape it repeatedly. This will particularly happen as the years go on and people experience more events in their lives. They may have learned more about the loved one and his/her death. Over time the story will change. For children and young adults who will carry the story with them for the rest of their lives, it is an important piece of their history and they should have an opportunity to revisit it as they need to. This can be done by talking with someone or writing it down.

For some people the story will not change, and they will continue to re-traumatize themselves with their telling of it. These bereaved people might be experiencing prolonged grief and need extra help along the road (like that of a therapist). Other people may only tell parts of the story to certain people. There may be the public story and the version reserved for family only or not told at all.

There are several basic questions I believe everyone should ask themselves as they grieve and feel overwhelmed with emotion (and look for help to ease that pain):

- What makes you feel better?
- What gets you through the day?

Sometimes in grief we only can think about getting through a minute at a time because the pain is so great. That pain will pass if we allow ourselves to think about how we can move ourselves through it. It is important that we acknowledge the hurt we feel, but what will get us off the couch or out of the chair where we feel stuck at the moment?

These can be very simple things. In fact, I think we have a tendency to believe that we have to make big changes to help ourselves cope with our losses. We do not. We simply need to reach inside ourselves and figure out what it is that can soothe us.

For instance, for some people it might be buying nail polish. Seeing a new color and its funny name makes us feel new and refreshed. And it is a reminder that there are still good things in the world. For other people, it could be moving from week to week, looking forward to a television show, knowing that a new episode will be on schedule in seven days after the most recent one.

Some people might be laughing, thinking, How can she believe that it could be that easy? But that is my point. We overthink grief so often when what we need to do is look out the window and realize that the sun is shining and it might be nice to sit in the sunshine for a while. And that gives us relief.

But we also should reflect back on other difficult points in our lives and ask ourselves:

- What helped us survive that event?
- Where did we find our strength?

The support we found in the past will offer clues about how to help ourselves.

Grief can be overwhelming. I'll be the first to admit that. I remember lying in bed in the mornings of the days and weeks after my sister died wondering how I could ever get up and face the day. And my days were filled with classes, papers to write, and college student newspaper activities. When we are overwhelmed, it means we need to slow down.

Take it a minute at a time if you need to. Maybe an hour at a time. Slow it down to whatever speed works for you. Make a list of items to accomplish in one day to give your brain a rest about what needs to be done. For a while you might not be able to do as much as you did. Grief is hard work, but if you cope with it now you will find that you can resume your usual speed later.

What you will find is that you will not need to take it a minute or an hour at a time later even though at some point you may have to repeat getting yourself through shorter periods of time. The point is recognizing when you feel overwhelmed by your feelings and giving those feelings a chance to emerge.

It also might not be about time but instead about taking a breather from whatever you are working on. You might need to do some relaxation through breathing. How grief overwhelms us is individual. Some people cannot shake images of the loved ones which then remind them of what they have lost while other people feel like they might never get past feeling so sad. After you have slowed down, then think about something that can help you cope. That is when all the ideas in this chapter come into play. And there might be something you can do that is not in this chapter or even in this book. Rocky Roads is a guide but only you know what can help you.

Be honest with each other. Changing a story to protect members of the family is not worth the long-range grieving it will cause the member of the family who has been told something else (or not told anything). No one does this out of malice, only to protect those they love from hurting more. Changing a different story, however, might lead someone to make up a story, which ultimately could be more damaging. And honesty during grief can promote a family's healing and trust.

Rituals and Grief Activities

While most people reading this book already have had a funeral or memorial, there still might be other grief activities that will happen as families embark on the suicide grief journey. These can be attending therapy and support groups or taking part in activities that the loved one enjoyed (all of which will be discussed below). There could be other remembrances or even awareness walks that come in time.

When these events happen, consider including grandparents, extended family, and friends who were close to the person (if it is geographically possible for them to attend). They might say no, they might not be interested, but more than likely, they will be grateful for being asked to take part. And opportunities like these can open communication barriers or give family members a chance to talk about what they have been through and what they remember about a loved one. Family members have an opportunity to dip into the pain of the loss as much as they can and then put it away. Activities like yearly walks or candlelight remembrances can become new family traditions.

In New Mexico, there is a yearly tradition of lighting luminarias (paper lunch bags filled with sand and candles, also known as farolitos) on Christmas Eve to light the way around homes. This was started as a way to light the spirit of the Christ child to one's home. But it is now a tradition that happens all around the United States. At some events, the names of loved ones who have died are written on the bags and they are lit as remembrances. A family might not do this as part of a large social gathering each year but it could become a small tradition for the family unit instead. Smaller grief activities can be born out of larger ones and serve to bring families together, even as the years go by.

Should my family get therapy?

This isn't a review of types of therapy available. That is not what this book is about. If you are interested in therapy, there are many books to read and people available with whom to discuss the possibilities. Instead, this is about sorting out if the family (and the individuals within it) should seek therapy. The information below is derived from a presentation I did with Jack Jordan in 2008 at the American Association of Suicidology Pre-Conference (Jordan, 2009). Jack is a therapist and discussed what people should look for in finding a therapist. Jack uses this approach when he speaks about coping with suicide loss.

Going to therapy is an individual and family decision. Therapy can be a great experience, and there are people who absolutely love it and will say it was the best decision they ever made. Other people find it does not work for them. What is significant is that there is no reason not to try therapy. One has nothing to lose. However, sometimes a particular therapist that can cause the experience not to be positive. That is why one should think about the points below before selecting a therapist.

Not all therapists have been trained to work in suicide grief. There is nothing wrong with shopping around or trying out therapists. This is one reason why people in therapy are sometimes referred to as "consumers"—you are buying the therapy so you really have a choice to pick the best therapist for you. The best way is to ask for referrals from other people for therapists who have worked with the suicide bereaved. Support groups for the bereaved by suicide are good for this because others in the group might have experience with a good local therapist (and can steer someone away from a bad therapist).

Do not continue to see a therapist who makes you feel bad for who you are and what you have been through. Evan a therapist who has experience working in suicide grief may have personal suicide-related issues (attempter, family member who died by suicide) that remain unresolved. These therapists need to cope with their issues before they can help others cope with suicide.

It is okay to ask therapists about their experience working with the suicide bereaved (or with people who have had traumatic losses). You need to know if they have experience helping the bereaved by suicide cope with some of the unique facets of suicide grief. Also, ask them about their experience of working with general grief and bereavement. It is good to work with a therapist who at least has experience with death and grief/bereavement if not suicide (and in a smaller community you may not have many choices of therapist).

In my experience as a workshop presenter, I often have therapists attend who want to know more about how to work with the suicide bereaved. They might have a current client or one in the past and they want to strengthen their skills. There are many therapists out there who truly want to help the suicide bereaved. Sometimes they just need the opportunity of good training to educate them. But understand that those who are working with you who might not have a lot of experience. They also might want to learn from you and use that to help people in the future (as well as helping you).

Can the therapist handle the intense pain (as well as the other emotions of suicide grief) and also realize that he or she will not know exactly how to guide individual bereaved people along the grief journey? It is a difficult balance. No therapist will be able to help all bereaved in the same way. There is no one size fits all for suicide grief.

The bereaved person should feel emotionally safe talking with the therapist. It is important to go with your intuition. If you do not feel that everything can be shared, it might be best to sever the relationship and look for another therapist. The bereaved person should not only feel secure but also have a sense that he or she will be supported in the healing journey he or she ultimately chooses.

One more time! Because of the importance of selecting the right therapist, it is okay to shop around and ask the therapist questions about his or her background. It is okay to go to a few sessions and then move on to another therapist if it is not working out. Your grief journey is at stake here and you want to know that the most helpful, supportive person is walking with you along the road. That means you do not always want to choose the first person who comes along. And that is okay.

How do you know when you should be going to therapy? Take a look at how you are coping. Are you happy with the direction you are going? Are you engaging in self-destructive behaviors like alcohol/drug abuse? Are you feeling depressed? Are you feeling suicidal? Or do you simply feel like you need someone to help guide you on your path? If you answered yes to any of these questions, then seek out a therapist. That person can give you the help you need and possibly help you place puzzle pieces together and connect events related to the loss that you are not able to do yourself.

Attending a Support Group for People Bereaved by Suicide

In the United States, the first support groups for people bereaved by suicide were started in the late 1970s. These groups were meant to bring people together who had lost a loved one to suicide, which was especially meaningful at the time because the prevalence of stigma surrounding suicide still left families hiding what had happened. For many people, a support group has been the place where for the first time they met other people bereaved by suicide.

Some groups are run as peer groups, meaning that a bereaved person leads the group. Others are professionally run, meaning a clinician is the leader. Still others are mutually led as peer-professional groups. In some places, these groups are closed: people must be placed into them and they run for a short period of time (several weeks) while others are drop-in groups where people can come periodically to a group that meets once or twice a month. There are no rules about what works best for any group. Some people go to groups and feel instantly at home while others do not believe the experience works for them (even after attending several times) and do not return. One feature of almost all groups is the sharing of experiences.

I believe groups are important for one simple reason: it is an opportunity to look around a room and say, "These are people just like me. These are people who have had the same kind of loss. I am not alone." It is okay to go to a group and just listen, too. Sometimes that is what people need.

But groups are not for everyone. And today, with the Internet, there are support groups online as well as ways to connect with people, not necessarily in a group or chat room setting, yet still making a link with another person coping with the same kind of loss. See the resources section for an on-line group that has existed on the Internet for over ten years.

Support group listings by state are available on the American Association of Suicidology and American Foundation for Suicide Prevention web sites. International listings can be found on the International Association for Suicide Prevention web site. Each organization's web site is listed in the resources section.

Bibliotherapy

For some people, books become a huge support. There is a lot of information available via books whether on suicide in general or about working through grief. Bibliotherapy is finding support through reading books. Some people might attend a support group but find books support them between group sessions or answer their questions between meetings. Other people cannot access support groups. Some people prefer reading about the experiences of other suicide bereaved and having the opportunity to revisit the book several times if they choose to.

Check out web sites for book reviews and recommendations. For instance, the American Association of Suicidology web site offers summaries only of books that have received favorable reviews from its publications review committee (which is made up of subject matter experts) and which are potentially beneficial for the intended audiences. If books are not recommended, they are not included. It is important to find books that create a sense of hope, and those that are reviewed and recommended can assure you of that.

Music

Many of us find music a source of comfort. Just think about the number of songs about coping with loss! We can relate to the lyrics or simply be soothed by the sound of the music. The resources section provides several suggestions of music written specifically about coping with loss.

Exercise

Grief is hard work. It is emotionally and physically draining. It makes us tired. And often the physical piece of that loss is left out. During grief, it is especially important to exercise. Do not be hard on yourself, but get out and go for a walk. Do not push yourself too hard; instead enjoy the season around you whether you watch leaves falling, trek through newly fallen snow, sense spring pop out, or stroll through the long shadows of an evening in summer.

Getting out of the house and surrounding ourselves with nature (as well as reconnecting with our physical environment) can do wonders for our mood and outlook.

And it does not have to be walking. We can swim lap upon lap in a pool, go for a hike or a bike ride. Or it could be yoga. And if you already exercise, do not stop because you are grieving. You need it now more than ever. It will help you re-establish equilibrium and contact with the earth.

Whatever you choose, use this time to let your mind wander. Let it float away to where it needs to go. There is something about the movement of the body that lets us think freely and find answers where we did not expect them, or find peace in what we cannot control. Or if you cannot let your mind wander, use the time to examine a specific task or difficulty in your life with which you are struggling. By taking the time to pull it apart and piece it back together, you might find the answer you need. The physical activity helps the brain find answers because it helps us let go.

Other Physical Activity

Obviously, exercise is not the only physical activity that we can do. Some of us have physically demanding jobs or home situations. A job might mean someone walks all day or is in constant motion in some way. And some people might have to chop wood to keep the house warm. Any type of physical activity is helpful.

Something like chopping wood also is a good way to cope with anger (obviously with safety in mind). There are people for whom physical expression is very important and might be the only way they can cope. If you have family members like this, you need to remember to respect that physical activity is the outlet they need to use. While I know you watch them from the window, wishing they would come in and sit down and talk with you, you have to let them travel their own road before they come back to you. And you can do this by letting them know you are there if they want to talk. Later in this chapter, I offer openers of how to engage someone in a conversation.

The Support of Pets

We might believe we know what will bond our families together during the loss of a loved one, but often it is what we least expect it to be. For some families, it might be the family pet. Animals can take the stress away, if only for a moment, through their antics and their needs to be walked and fed.

While I do not recommend that everyone who experiences a suicide loss run out and adopt a pet, I do believe that pets provide something in our lives that we often do not realize we have until we experience a loss. My dissertation research was on the ways people use dogs to help them cope with the death loss of a loved one. My major finding was that even people satisfied with the human supports in their lives found that the dogs gave them something more.

This support could simply have been that the dog was there when they came home from work to greet them and let them pet it while they cried and talked about how much they missed their loved one. People needed that link with the deceased loved one. Just like a child, the pet needs care and attention and provides a reason to get out of bed in the morning. Some people pointed out that the dog made them laugh with its antics. And for others, going for a walk forced them to get out into the physical environment, exercise, and sometimes talk to people they met along the way. As each member of the family is unique, pets are, too, and they have a role in the family. If we allow them to, they are ready to be supports through our losses as well.

Crying

People often ask about crying. We have a taboo around crying in our western society. We act as if it is bad, and we think it makes people appear weak. Crying is a very natural part of life and our emotions. We need to cry to let those emotions go. Often, we realize after crying that we feel much better. It is an emotional expression. However, it is also important to remember that some people might not cry. While we worry about family members, wondering why they do not cry, we should step back and think about whether they have cried in past situations. It might be that crying is not a form of emotional expression for them and that they have another method of coping. People also worry about crying in public.

I told the story about Iris Bolton running out of the grocery store when she saw her son Mitch's favorite cereal in the breakfast foods aisle. The panic that Iris felt is probably familiar to all of us at one time or another. It is that fight-or-flight way of coping with stress, and this time we have chosen to flee. We fear what others will think if we sob over a box of cereal. The reality is that anyone who has had a loss will be able to relate. Maybe it was not a box of cereal that caused someone else to cry and flee; perhaps it was a favorite beverage or potato chips. We do not have to fear crying in front of others. It might seem that we cannot stop crying, that the crying is going on forever, but it will not as long as we continue on the journey. I have heard of people who allow themselves to cry at certain times of day when they are alone. For some people, this works really well (if they can cry on demand). Others need to be aware of triggers so we can prepare ourselves. This does not mean to stuff our feelings inside us but to allow them to flow and not panic if we are in a public place.

Self-Expression

Positive self-expression is significant in grief and there are many individual ways we can express ourselves in our pain for our loss.

Writing a book about my sister's suicide was never in my goals, though I had wanted to be writer since I was six years old. But when she died, and I had little access to other bereaved-by-suicide siblings (in 1993 the Internet barely existed), writing a book felt like one way I could tell my story and reach other siblings. However, I remind people when I am speaking that writing a book is a lofty goal. For some people writing their story can be a great way to "let it out" and find meaning. Sometimes writing is a way for us to find answers. It has been for me through the years. Letter writing was part of my life before email was available. There are many ways we can write. For instance, keeping a journal can be helpful. We can do it as a way of telling our story over time or putting our emotions down on paper (or on the computer) to let them go. We can write fiction or memoirs about our experiences. Think about how many times novels and memoirs recount the death (not always a suicide) of a loved one and the far-reaching effects of that loss on the author's life. Writing letters to our deceased loved one is a good way to say to them all that we did not get the opportunity to tell them when they were living.

Some people choose art as a means of expression. It could be a painting or a piece of pottery. People make quilts out of their loved ones' clothing—a way for their loved ones to surround them.

Other bereaved people create gardens, planting flowers that the loved ones enjoyed. For children, it might be as simple as putting together a puzzle that they often did with the person who died. Children also can put together a memory box of the person they loved. It can be a simple wooden box they decorate (with paint or other materials) and it can include items that remind them of the loved one: a swatch from a piece of the person's clothing, ticket stubs of events they attended together, and photos. Children should be guided in this activity and given suggestions of items to include as well as the opportunity to share the significance of the items and the experience.

Another way for people to express themselves is by giving in some way to charity through time or energy. This could be by creating quilts for children in hospitals or helping build houses for low-income families. Maybe your loved one had an organization he or she liked to work with and you can continue that tradition for him or her.

It might not come easy, a way to express oneself in grief. Give yourself time and reflect on your relationship with that person. What was important to you both? What kinds of things did you like doing together? What kinds of things do you like to do?

An Unfinished Project/Hobby

Figuring out how to honor our loved one's memory can take time. We have to sort through our relationship and what was important to them as well as what is important to us. I often tell people to think about the loved one's hobbies or if they had any volunteer work they liked to do, and build on that. Doing something they enjoyed is a way of keeping our bond with them.

There might be an unfulfilled project or dream that can be accomplished to honor the person's memory. Tony Gee and his daughters Alex and Bee in Australia lost their daughter/younger sister Nellie to suicide when she was fifteen, in 2005. Nellie loved ice hockey and had been invited to train with the Australian women's team. One of her dreams had been to skate on a frozen lake in Canada. Because she never fulfilled it, Tony and the girls plan to take a trip to Canada for what would have been Nellie's twenty-first birthday in 2010 and live out the dream for her. While flying across an ocean is not always feasible, sometimes keeping the loved one's dream alive is a way for us to honor them and keep our hope afloat. There might be ways we can do this closer to home.

Other people choose to do charity work in memory of the loved one. In addition to being active in be a cause that was important to the loved one, consider working in the suicide prevention/postvention field.

Advocacy

For some bereaved people, helping prevent suicide or working with other bereaved people is a way they believe they can help their loved one's memory live on and help other bereaved families. There are many ways to advocate. The Suicide Prevention Action Network USA was built on the grassroots advocacy of people bereaved by suicide. Jerry and Elsie Weyrauch started the organization after their medical doctor daughter, Teri, died by suicide. The Weyrauchs ran the organization out of their basement, and for years those of us involved collected paper petitions and then gathered in Washington, DC, to deliver them to our congressional representatives and discuss the importance of mental health parity and funding for suicide prevention.

While SPAN USA is now a part of the American Foundation for Suicide Prevention (AFSP), and the paper petitions have been replaced by the Internet, the bereaved can still make a difference at the grassroots level in their communities. Often it is the bereaved (particularly in the United States) who have made funding and awareness happen.

Get an education on suicide and survivorship. Get involved with a local support group or suicide prevention coalition. It is a starting point. The people who have been leading the groups usually know people who work in the prevention and postvention areas. There also are local contacts available on the SPAN USA web site and the Suicide Prevention Resource Center by state (see resources). These groups will give you some ideas of how you can help in your community.

Activities include workshops and education for all groups of people; everyone should know the warning signs of suicide, how to ask if someone is suicidal, and what to do after the person responds. There also are awareness events. September 10 each year is World Suicide Prevention Day. AFSP sponsors National Suicide Survivors Day the Saturday before Thanksgiving each year in the United States. Awareness events are often local walks or candle lightings to remember people who have died by suicide.

Each state in the United States has at least one Faces of Suicide Quilt. These quilts were started in the mid-1990s by Sandy Martin, whose son had died by suicide. Her idea came from the AIDS quilts, which gave her the idea that people needed to see the faces of those who died by suicide. Stigma historically lets people believe that those who die by suicide are not like everyone else. Obviously, that is not true, and Sandy wanted people to see that people who die by suicide can be your neighbor, your child's best friend, or your own family member. The quilts are taken to congressional meetings and displayed at events and libraries in various communities. People in Australia recently created their country's first quilt.

But creating the quilts is also a means of expression and advocacy for the people who construct squares in memory of their loved ones. These squares are as unique as the person who died. Some organizations have come together to create the squares in groups, giving the bereaved a chance to laugh, cry, and remember while also expressing their grief and love for someone they cared about.

Sandy and I conceived the colors purple and turquoise as the colors for the cause of suicide. We chose two colors because every cause appears to have one color and because turquoise is known as a healing color and we felt that purple complimented it well. While we initially started it to support the bereaved, we realized it really encompassed the entire issue of suicide and use the colors as much as possible when doing any work related to suicide. We have tried to spread the word through fabric ribbon pins or metal ribbon pins that people can wear. The colors appear on the cover of this book.

Wearing a purple and turquoise pin is a small but empowering way that people can educate others about suicide. Part of advocacy is telling our story; letting people know that suicide can happen to anyone; and sharing with them how they can help someone in pain or grieving. However, this public face does not suit everybody.

Working with bereaved people is another kind of advocacy. It is letting people know that they are not alone. Or it is giving back where someone else (or a group) helped you. It does not have to be through a support group but instead can be by acting as an available network if someone needs someone to talk to while grieving.

What is difficult about advocacy is helping the bereaved understand that they must grieve first before they can give back. I was lucky that someone I knew from high school who became a therapist told me early on to make sure that I took care of myself first before I tried to help others because otherwise I would not be much help. I have watched people who are desperate to make their pain stop and make sense of the road they are on, and think that the only way to do it is through advocacy. I tell people who contact me shortly after their loved ones die that we want them around for the long run, not the short run. I tell them to take care of themselves first and then return to me when they have done that.

It has been suggested that the bereaved wait two years before they can advocate. Knowing that the grief journey is individual, I do not believe there is a fixed time limit for any person. It is good to talk with someone to get a sense if you are in a place where you can help others. People who do not take the time to grieve the loss of the loved one sometimes burn out and then come to a complete halt with their advocacy work. Burnout can stall whatever they were working on and can grind a movement to a halt. I tell people we want to see them for a long time, not a short time.

Advocacy is usually different for siblings and parents. Siblings usually have to carry their losses through a large portion of their lives and might not choose to be as involved as their parents. They might never want to be involved in advocacy, instead choosing other ways to remember their deceased sibling. Their wishes should be respected, just as they should allow their parents to do the work they believe they need to do for others.

Engaging Family Members

It is not easy to engage all family members in a discussion about the loved one. There are times when we want to talk about our deceased loved one, when we feel a need to remember something or tell others something we found out about them. But when we start talking, we can see that they do not want to "go there." They do not want to be a part of the discussion. As mentioned before, there are times when we watch a loved one go outside to chop wood or even read a book rather than talking with us.

We have to remember that not everyone wants to talk about it. Nor does everyone want to talk about it at the same time. While we might feel the need to discuss the person, another family member might express himself or herself differently, maybe through writing in a notebook.

It is always worth a try to engage family members. The best way to go about it is to keep the lines of communication open. Let them know that you're available at any time to talk—but understand that they might not want to talk to you. They may need to find other people to talk with (outside the family, if needed) who are willing to act as listening supports.

Part of keeping the lines of communication open includes sharing our own grief. People sometimes believe that they need be strong for their other family members (particularly children), but children need to see their parents grieving. Parents are the role models for children, and if children see their parents grieving, then they will know it is okay to cry and talk about the loved one.

Here are some lines we can use to let family members know the lines of communication are open:

"Do you remember the time when all of us . . . ?" Or "Do you remember when . . .did . . . ?"

"I have been feeling a little sad lately. Have you been feeling it, too?"

"I've been thinking about [our loved one] a lot recently. What about you?"

"There is a remembrance event coming up. Would you like to take part?"

It is also important to acknowledge the steps family members have made in coping with their grief. For instance, after they have shared something about their grief, let them know that you appreciate their sharing with you. Acknowledging it can boost their confidence about how they are coping. Sometimes encouragement from people we care about is all we need to know that we are making progress in our grief.

What If I Am Worried About a Family Member?

The death of a loved one, particularly by suicide, can make us more aware of our loved ones. It also can make us paranoid, not wanting to let those around us out of our sight because we fear losing them as well. It is important when we are concerned about our loved ones to take a step back and make sure that their behavior has changed rather than our grief reaction of fear leading to overprotection.

However, some family members do exhibit signs of needing help. Sometimes they are reaching for help but are not sure how to do it and instead choose unhealthy coping mechanisms (like substance abuse, cutting themselves to release the pain, or a change in eating habits). We should be aware of our loved ones and how they are coping. If their behavior has changed and/or they are showing signs of unhealthiness, then reach out to them. Earlier in the book, in the chapter on suicide, we discussed the warning signs of suicide. After there has been one suicide in the family, there is no such thing as reaching out too many times and making sure everyone is okay. National resource information for the United States and other countries is listed in the resource section of the book. It is a start to find a local or regional resource although you also could Google your community and "suicide prevention" or another series of keywords to see what local resources are listed on the Internet.

What Do We Do with Their Belongings?

After someone dies, we are left with a room full (or even a house full) of their belongings. Sorting through them can be distressing and difficult. I do not believe there is one right answer for any family. We took our time sorting through Denise's stuff. The word *stuff* is putting it mildly because my sister had saved everything right down to her dental appointment cards. Today all that is left of her physical life is a trunk full of items that we have chosen to save to remember her life. These things are symbolic of a life that has ceased physical existence. They can include clothes and belongings as well as photos and videos. These objects are important, particularly right after the death, because we cling to them as all we have left to remember the loved one by. We know we have the memories but as we integrate the loss of the physical person, we cling to physical objects to help us cope. As we progress, we will not feel the need to hold onto as many items.

It took almost a year to part with everything because we did it in phases. Some families might not have the luxury of taking the time to sort through items if a move is in place because a family's financial situation has changed. If the person lived alone, the dwelling where they lived needs to be emptied. What is important is that families keep some items to remember the person by. It is better to give away less in the beginning and part with it later than to give everything away and be sorry later. Items usually can be stored for some time.

The time spent going through the belongings of the loved one can be very healing in itself. It can be a time of remembering why a particular T-shirt or music CD was bought. It can be a time where stories are shared and good memories previously not known to other family members are passed around. For some people, the smell of the person retained on the clothing is part of the memory of that person. This experience can bring family members together and also help them to explore the life of the loved one whom no one wants to forget and whom everyone needs to understand in some way. All family members might not want to be involved, although everyone should be encouraged to take part just as in any rituals and grief activities following the death.

When a family turns the person's room into a shrine, or when one person refuses to let go of the way things were before the person died, then family members will need to help that person slowly part with the items. It is difficult when there is denial that the person has died and a family member believes the person still might need their clothes. Such denial suggests complicated grief, in which outside help is needed for much more than helping to sort through the belongings of the loved one.

Coping with Holidays

Holidays can be difficult enough without the added pressure of coping with a family member who has died by suicide. Bringing family together for any occasion can be traumatic, taking them back to holidays throughout their lives that might not have been happy. But it also can be a time for healing.

It can be meaningful for a family to take some time early in the day to acknowledge the person who is no longer physically present. This can be done through lighting a candle, saying a prayer, or going to the cemetery. Some people set a place at the table for the person. Whatever the remembrance, it should be something that can defuse the tension in the family by reminding them that while the loved one is not present for the holiday, he or she is still part of the family unit.

A great example of how a family can find healing is in the short film *THAW: Christmas at the Cemetery* (see the resource section). While it's a fictional film, it is one family's journey from the depths of division to finding its way back together again. Jeff Orgill, the filmmaker, based it on his mother's experience after the loss of her other son, Jeff's brother. The film shows a family divided on Christmas morning. No one is communicating except to pick at each other. On the way to taking the father to the airport (which indicates the marriage has ended), the mother makes a stop at the cemetery. From the back of the van, she pulls out a Christmas tree and places it by the brother's grave. Realizing she forgot the ornaments, she uses the bag of aluminum cans she has brought along to drop off for recycling. One by one, the other members of the family join her in decorating the tree, probably the first time since the brother's death they have worked together to do anything.

The film shows how families divide after the suicide and how the deceased member still affects the family, even though he or she is not part of the family physically anymore. Finally, it shows how a family can find some common ground where they can join back together, if only slowly and for a short time at first.

All steps are taken slowly. The road might seem slow here. It might seem as if steps are taken backward after some forward movement is made. Remember that coming back together will not be quick. Each family member needs to be in the same place at some point. Enjoy the time when it happens and allow everyone to separate as needed. It is no different from the times when we feel overwhelmed with grief and we cry and let go. Then we need to go and do something else for a while, watch a movie or go for a walk. The family is the same. The family comes together for a time and then each member must go off and do his or her work alone for a while.

Finding a Family's Strength

It will not necessarily be easy for a family to see what its strength is because what works for one family will not work for another. It will take some time for the family (or one person in the family, probably the one reading this book) to search through the family itself to find what holds it together.

Several years ago I was speaking at the International Association for Suicide Prevention conference in Ireland. I was discussing the importance of a family finding the strength somewhere to cope. One woman from Sweden, a therapist, raised her hand and said she needed help with that because she could not see how many families in Sweden would be able to do that because they are separated in many ways (geographically, by divorce, and so forth).

A woman from the United States pointed out that the family had shared a history and that perhaps coming back together and remembering the good times could be the strength. She suggested using photo albums. Even if the strength is in the past, it is still part of the family. Photo albums might help family members remember the good times they had with the person and with each other.

The family should draw on the values and traditions that hold it together and make it a system. It might take time to locate the strengths in a family that has been devastated by suicide, but in time, a family will find them. Sometimes Jews say "may his [or her] memory be a blessing" when mentioning the name of someone who has died. It will take some searching to find that blessing, but it is there. Possibly new traditions will be created. Without one family member, some of the traditions will not be the same and families might look to celebrate the holidays differently while others will want to cling to what they have done in the past.

The Continued Bond

Death does not sever our bonds with those we love. The bond simply changes because the dead are no longer physically here with us. They still are part of our lives and they affect the decisions we make and who we continue to evolve into.

For a long time in grief therapy, it was recommended that people sever the bond and the attachment with the person who died. It was believed that this was the best way to cope. I am thankful that this approach has gone out of style (and that I was not aware of it when my sister died). When I am speaking in public,

I often talk about how I have always had a sense of my sister being with me. I can honestly say that I do not believe there was ever a time when I did not feel her presence and her guiding and leading me to help others. But I also have gone almost as much of my life without her as I did with her as I was only twenty-one when she died.

Many people whose loved ones have died have experienced some sort of sign that the loved one is still with them. It can be a butterfly, a song on the radio that plays at just the right time, finding a coin (pennies from heaven as they are known), or something else that is significant in the relationship between those two people. If you believe in these signs, be thankful for them and they will continue to come. They can provide assurance that our loved ones are near even though the connection has changed.

Finding Meaning

Death does not make sense to us. We are taught to live life to its fullest, that life is sacred, and that we should not take ours or that of another person's. When someone dies, we are left to yearn for the physical presence that is no longer there. We cry because there will be no new memories. We wonder what our lives mean when they ended theirs.

We need to make meaning of the death and how that loss affects our lives. We do this by traveling the road of grief. Finding meaning in a suicide death might be more difficult than finding meaning in other kinds of death because suicide does not follow the natural order in life. Again, because we are taught that life is sacred, we do not understand how someone we cared so much for could end his or her life.

But before we can find that meaning along the road, we have to cope with the loss itself. We have to feel it, live it, and let it flow through us. We have to cope and accept how our loved one died. We have to cope with how it reflects on our lives. While you may not feel able to do that from where you are standing, know that one day you will look back and see that you do get it. You will get to that place in the road. You will not know where it is until you reach it, and the meaning might surprise you. But that does not matter because it is what it is supposed to be for you.

If there are people who want to help you along the way, let them. They might help you find meaning where you could not put ideas together. Because grief is taxing, you might miss some ideas or thoughts. By listening, other people can see the ideas and add them up and present them back to you.

But if you are traveling the road alone, that is okay, too. Maybe you will meet someone along the way, a fellow bereaved person, or someone else who might come into your life. Or it might be someone who re-enters your life to help you through this experience. You can do this. You might want to stop and rest sometimes. That is okay. But do not give up. Do not let the road intimidate you. Somewhere along the way are the answers that you seek and that you need. I know because I have been there and watched many people walk unique roads. Whatever it is supposed to be, it will unroll itself in front of you if you let it.

Finally, remember your deceased loved one is with you on the road, too. While you might not be able to see him or her, they are with you in some way, whatever way you believe them to be. It may simply be in your memories of them or it could be through the signs they send you. What matters most is that you acknowledge their presence and use it as strength to help you continue forward in this journey.

Remember, they do not want you to hurt. They do not want you to go through life unhappy because they died. They want you to smile and be happy and enjoy the life in front of you. They want you to be fulfilled. They could not see beyond their own pain but that does not mean that they wanted you to hurt, too. They want you to remember them for the good times you shared together, the laughter, the great memories. And they want you to use all that as the hope to give you the energy to lift you up and keep you going.

12. Checking the Map

Road maps are not always easy to read. Some people read them better than others. So how do we know when we are going in the right direction?

In time, the pain will subside even though it does not feel like it now. There are a lot of emotions. For some people, there are years of anger and frustration toward the person (and other family members) that leak out. Everything under the surface becomes visible. It is not easy. No rocky road is. However, a rocky road can be traveled. And it can change and smooth out. Each note I make below is what I hope for you and your family as you take your healing journeys both separately and together.

Some markers that help us know that physically and emotionally we are regaining a sense of a new normal include the regularization of our eating and sleeping habits. Grief is very taxing and might have made us more tired and more or less hungry. We also will find that we are not thinking about the person every minute of the day as we might have been previously. We usually do not even realize it has happened. Suddenly, we might be thinking about the weather or laughing about a joke and then think about it. Contrary to the fear many people have, this does not mean we are forgetting our loved one. It just means we are integrating them into our lives in a different way. And not a bad way; it is just different from what it was.

One time I was eating lunch with a group of bereaved people after a meeting. At this particular restaurant, I always get a cookie with my meal because I like the cookies so much. As we were waiting for our food, I was nibbling on the cookie and someone asked why I was eating my cookie before my meal when a recent survivor of suicide loss piped in, "Haven't you learned from this to eat your dessert first?" That is what suicide teaches us: enjoy the life we still have and live it fully.

In prevention, we often talk about finding the life side—how do we help someone find those reasons to live? In postvention, it is much the same. After a suicide, they are there. They might be fleeting at first, a wave of happiness that goes as quickly as it comes, but in time the waves are longer and come back stronger than the waves of sadness and loss. We can find ways of reconnecting with our lost loved one without wanting to end our own lives to be with them. It takes time to find those ways, but we can do it.

There will come a time when the bereaved separate how the loved ones died from who they were in life. This is a huge step forward in grief. The bottom line is that we do not have to suffer in grief. Our loved ones do not want us to suffer. They want us to go on and live rich, happy lives filled with sunshine and laughter.

I still believe my sister is my biggest cheerleader in my life. I have a sense that she is with me as I travel through life, that she is helping me to accomplish whatever I set out to do and that she knows that the Michelle who lost a sister at twenty-one is still there and can accomplish the things I want to do. While I speak and write about her death and work in several facets of the suicide prevention field, I do not think about her in the way she died. I remember who she was in the life she lived. I remember the good times we had and all that we shared. Everyone can get there. There is no reason why people cannot. We only are held back by ourselves.

I believe many people who have experienced the death (not only suicide) of someone they care about have an equally strong sense of the presence of their loved one in daily life. Still feeling connected to that person in our lives gives us hope. No matter what we believe about the afterlife, feeling that someone we care about is with us in some way might be the one thing that keeps us going each day. I also strongly believe that our loved ones send us signs to let us know that they are near. Be aware of these. Embrace them. A sense of connectedness, especially for the bereaved by suicide, is a marker that a loved one is not in pain or suffering as they were in the physical world.

There will be bad days (road bumps) in the grief experience. We often call them the peaks and valleys of grief or say that it comes in waves. But that is okay. You might get frustrated because you believe you have been doing well and then one day you think you have taken a giant step backward. You really have not. Grief sometimes washes over you when you least expect it. Get to know the triggers. Do you hear songs on the radio that remind you of that person? Is it a day that is significant? You might not even be aware of what is setting you off until you take a step back. Instead of letting the triggers make you feel bad, embrace them. Think of them as reminders that your loved one is with you in some way and wants you to remember the good times.

Loss is difficult no matter how you slice it. We get sad when we lose material items like a favorite sweater or our cell phone. Losing a job or a friend, or the end of the marriage or a move due to unfortunate circumstances—all are situations where we feel that something has been taken from us. When we lose a loved one, that emptiness reaches even deeper inside us. It feels almost as if we have lost a piece of our core being.

Somehow we have to find a way to fill that empty spot up again, a way that is satisfying to us for the long term. There are many ways to do that, discussed throughout this book. But we also have to remember that we can use the loss as a catalyst to be better people, to have better relationships with our loved ones in the future, and to serve as a reminder of the pain we do not want to endure again.

We do that by communicating with our loved ones (and that includes anyone we care about in our lives), letting them know we care about them, but also telling them when we are worried about them. When we are worried, we do not let them walk away, we make sure they clearly understand we are there for them. While we cannot control the decisions that other people choose to make, what we can control is knowing that we did everything possible we could in that moment. We want to learn from our mistakes, and the loss has given us that chance. We do not want to waste it.

Life does not give us the opportunity to rewind and do over. Instead, we are given chances to make changes in our own lives. We can start over with loved ones, like our families and other people we care about. We can forge new bonds. We can make sure we do not miss out again. Our loved ones' suicides tell us not to take anything for granted. We can help other people understand what to look for if they are worried about someone they love. We have choices.

It is also important that after a loved one dies by suicide, we do not deny it. We do not put on a happy face and act like nothing is wrong when really we are breaking inside. What are we proving by doing that? Grief needs the chance to flow. It is like a wound that will not heal. It keeps bleeding because it is not given the healing energy that it needs. It needs to process. Once it can process, it then starts to scab. The more the grief is denied, the more it bleeds. And if the wound is smothered, grief will find another way to work itself out, usually as a not-very-pleasant physical illness.

Having grown up in Illinois, I always tell people grief reminds me of cornfields. When we are driving along a road, they appear to go on forever without a road to turn onto. We cannot wait and try to maneuver around the cornfields. We have to cut right through them. That is how we work through grief.

Two other markers tell me people have moved forward in their grief (and are headed in the right direction on the road): when they are able to let go of the guilt and the "whys?" Guilt is time- and energy-consuming. I have watched people pace rooms at support groups because they could not move past what they felt they could have, would have, and should have done. I have heard from people around the world who scratch their heads constantly and want to go back and redo events in their lives, thinking they can change circumstances. We all do. And we feel bad for the mean things we told someone. But we make headway on our healing journey when we finally can tell ourselves we have done all we can and it is time to let it go.

And we cannot think about the "whys?" forever. We wonder what signs we missed. We comb their belongings for clues; we ask their friends and all our loved ones about what they remember and if they saw something we did not; we read everything we can on suicide and mental illness and any other related subject, believing the answers are there. At some point, we have to let it go. We have to realize that while here on this earth, we will never truly know why. And we have to be okay with that.

Some of the most difficult moments in a family come when our bereaved loved ones do not want to move forward with us. I have talked to many siblings in particular over the years who wanted to move forward but their parents were stuck somewhere else on the road. The parents were afraid to go forward because they feared that going forward meant having to let go of the person who died. This is a misconception. Letting them go does not mean we let go of the memories and our love for them. How could that be possible? How could you let go of many years of memories and love as if you were taking out the trash or giving up a bad habit?

People were led to believe in the past that once a person died, they had to sever the bond, the tie that held them together. This is not true. There is a lot of emotional comfort in retaining the bond. The key is that we have to process how the relationship has changed and in what way we can retain a bond with our loved one's absence from our physical world. They remain part of our everyday world although in a different way since they are no longer physically present.

When we let their physical presence go, we set our previous bond free to make a new kind of bond in this "new normal" that we have formed.

But if our family does not want to do that, if our family does not want to attend the support group, go on the walk, or discuss the suicide, then we need to reach beyond that system to do it. Think about the people in the suprasystem, on the outside, waiting to help. They want to contribute in some way and this is their chance. Reach out to them. It is like forging new bonds because the opportunity is there.

This does not mean letting go of your family. It just means you have chosen to move forward when other family members might not be ready. That is okay.

No one else is responsible for you. No one else can take care of us. And no one should hold us back. The hope is that one day they will be ready, and they might be ready when they see that even though you have moved forward, you have not let go of the loved one, that that person is still just as much a part of your life as he or she was when he or she was alive. It is just a different kind of relationship. And they will see that you are laughing and smiling and you are doing it because you know that your loved one is with you. Think of it as leading by example.

However we choose to cope with our grief, it involves telling the story of our loved one. This does not always mean that we go to a support group or we write it (two of the more common ways people use to tell the story). We could be processing it through a walk or chopping wood. Think of it as a picture. You are taking the time to paint the story which then allows you to reframe it and place it somewhere new. Telling the story, however you do it, may help you to understand an aspect of the loved one that you did not realize was there up to now. Finally, in time, after telling the story what seems like millions of times, you are able to let go of the pieces of it that you no longer need.

My hope is that you can let go of how your loved one died and focus on the happy memories that you had with that person. I hope you reach a point where you can see you are being given an opportunity to remember your loved one in a way that is important and special to you. Think about what was important in your relationship and what you can do to remember this person. If you allow your mind to wander through those years of memories and the importance of your relationship, you will figure it out. You just have to give yourself a chance to get there.

Some books talk about "grief recovery" or "recovering from loss." I am not sure that these words are adequate. While I believe that grief is a normal part of life, I also believe in integrating the grief and the life of the loved one into our current life. Recovery, to me, is about going back to who we were. But we will also be someone new because the loss has changed us.

Within the system, each subsystem and each family member also will need to grieve separately from the rest of the family. Each person will be in a different place in his or her grief from the moment he or she learns that the loved one has died. It will be important to respect those differences and work through one's own grief so that the family can come together.

Stories will be different within the family. Needs will be different. Once family members recognize this, each person can find the space needed to grieve. And within this reorganization, a renegotiation of the loss within the family needs to happen. We have to come to agreement on what it means to the family unit. It might be somewhat different to us as individuals because of our unique relationships with the person who died, but the family unit needs its own meaning.

Not all families will have the ability to come back together. If a family suffered from severe dysfunction before the loss, it might be too difficult to restore much hope. However, for the family members who choose to move forward in their lives, outlets are available in the suprasystem to help them on their grief journeys. Suicide can hinder the normal development of the family, but it does not have to be that way.

What might be most difficult for families after a suicide is forgiveness. Not only do we have to forgive our loved ones for leaving us (and choosing, in some way, to do so), we also have to forgive ourselves for where we believed we failed in their lives. Finally, we need to forgive the family members we might blame or believe added to the reasons the person ended up killing him or herself. Forgiveness is not easy and involves being able to let go of what hurts us. And forgiveness is not always reciprocal. We might forgive a family member but that other person might not want to forgive us. When this happens, we know we have done what we need to do and we need to be okay with that. Most important, and something we often forget during grief: just because people need to grieve differently does not mean they do not love each other.

Some family members who so badly want to reconnect with the loved one might think about attempting suicide themselves. They will need extra support at this time in learning to move forward in a life-sustaining way and realizing they do not have to forget the loved one who has died.

Rituals can help family members with structure. Look at the everyday small rituals like reading the morning paper with our spouse, petting the dog, or watching a certain television show with our children. Those rituals provide structure and comfort in our lives.

Within values and traditions, the importance of ceremonies and rituals cannot be overstated. Grief is hindered without them. Sometimes in suicide, because of the stigma and the concept that a life is cut short, ceremonies and rituals are bypassed. But this is the time when they are most important. The survivors need validation that their loved ones are okay, that their loved one will go where they believe they should be. And everyone needs a chance to say goodbye in whatever way they need to.

In our families, it is much the same. While we all need our time and space to grieve, we also need to grieve with our families. One of us is gone and the pie has to be reconfigured. We still need to keep a piece of the pie because that person has not left our family completely. He or she is still part of it, yet our loved one will not have the same place as in the past. The slices are now cut for the members who are left because we still have a share in the family. We are still part of something greater, a system that needs us. The system might seem chaotic, as if it has lost its way. Or perhaps the system was somewhat messy before the loss.

The system can find its way, though. We need to draw on the strengths of the family. Just as we need to find reasons to live, so do the pieces of the family need to be pulled back together. Those strengths will be unique to each family and time must be taken to find them. They are there, though. When they are found, reach for them and use them.

Suicide rewrites the futures of all whose lives are touched by it. But by recognizing that we are different people, that our grief experiences will be unique, we can work through our grief, and our families can emerge stronger than before. Any family, with work, can rally in times of crisis and can grow and transform itself from the stress of the loss. Just as the scenery along a road changes as we travel from one place to another, so will our perspective as we move through grief and reach the different stops and overlooks along the way.

13. Notes for Caregivers, Clinicians, Friends, and Other Supports

If you want to help someone you care about who is bereaved by suicide, your first concern is to examine your own view of death and then your view of suicide. You must understand your own attitudes and beliefs before you can help other people.

As a twenty-one year old when my sister died, I had a hard time understanding that some people in my life reacted as they did because of their own experiences with suicide. It took me about ten years to fully comprehend this idea, and it happened by means of a friendship with someone I worked with at the *Ball State Daily News*. Although I knew his family had not been healthy, I did not remember that he had shared long before Denise died that his father had been suicidal at various times, often putting the family in harm's way. When Denise died and he backed away from me, it was sad to me because he was someone I worked with every day and considered a good friend. Our friendship was never the same although we worked together for about six more months. It ultimately severed a friendship and led to me leaving the newspaper during my senior year.

If you have experience with suicide in your past, please do not be afraid of the person you care about who is walking a grief journey. Share your story with them (or with someone else if you are not that comfortable) and let them know you have not abandoned them. They will appreciate your honesty and the opportunity to travel with you as you maneuver through your own life experience.

Not only should you be aware of your own experiences with death and suicide, but you also should understand the positive and negative emotions you have around them. Where do they come from? Why do you feel that way? Once you have spent time exploring them, you then can move on to helping others. It is imperative never to allow your own emotions to block how you help someone. This is particularly true for the suicide bereaved who already might have encountered a therapist/clinician/loved one who is uncomfortable with the topic and made it very clear to the bereaved. This validates the shame and stigma that the bereaved person is trying to overcome. Instead, be open to what the bereaved need you to hear. They might not know exactly how they need help but in listening to them, you can piece it together and help them understand where they are on the healing journey and where they need to go.

For the family that has lost someone to suicide, acknowledgment from the community is extremely important to their healing. While it is not expected that people will come and smother the family with casseroles (there really are only so many casseroles families can eat—think about how welcome a pizza might be one night!), it does help when people hear from their neighbors, and all the communities involved in their lives (work, school, neighborhood, church, and so forth). These communities are where we do most of our routine functioning, and to know that the community cares, is aware of what has happened and that it is devastating to the family, helps particularly after suicide because of the shame and stigma surrounding it.

Different people will offer help to each person who is grieving. Some people will have extended family members who come to help. Other people might live far away from extended families and instead may get help from neighbors. While the families appreciate any help they get after the loss, most of all they appreciate the acknowledgment of the loss.

As I discussed earlier, the Internet has changed the way we grieve. People have places where they can reach out as never before. It is not just about status reports on Facebook that indicate someone has died, but there are also opportunities to talk about how much we miss the loved one and to share anniversaries as they approach. People want to know others are there for them and feeling their pain of the loss. While I was working on this book, I sometimes would ask for comments from my Facebook friends about various issues relating to this book. One day I asked those bereaved by suicide the one thing they wished they had known about the suicide grief journey that they now understand. Most people responded that they wished they had known they did not have to travel the grief journey alone.

Because of the stress when someone dies, people often need to be guided and shown what to do. Families need one person to take a leadership role and manage everything, down to making sure that dinner gets on the table and the laundry is done. This does not need to happen forever but it helps for at least the first few weeks to have some extra help. Or if one person can manage the people who want to offer more emotional and practical support, that is even better. The list of ways people can help is endless: bringing meals (those that can be frozen and then baked in the oven are very helpful; that way the family can access them as needed, especially on the bad days when dinner is almost impossible to get to the table); getting the children to and from school; answering phone calls and taking messages; cleaning the house/doing dishes/helping with the laundry; and anything else that might be important that the family is having a difficult time accomplishing.

I still have not forgotten the man who left a bag filled with paper plates, napkins, and plastic utensils on my family's doorstep after Denise died. I remember seeing him drive away and the card that he left. He said he did not know us but he felt like he needed to do something for us. And it helped not to have to worry about washing dishes for a few days. Often, the most appreciated gestures are so simple they do not even occur to us.

Sometimes the bereaved are not sure how to reach out for help. They might do it in what we consider strange or disconcerting ways like showing signs of suicidal ideation themselves. Do not be afraid to ask them if they are suicidal. When someone is suicidal, it is very difficult for people to reach out to the people in pain. People are afraid to ask. But by being afraid to ask, they are risking that person's life when what that person really wants is someone to throw a life preserver from the shore and let them know they can survive and make it back to land. If you ask, you really will not offend someone or put ideas into their heads, but you might save a life.

The chapter on suicide earlier in the book talks about the warning signs of suicide. It gives people an idea of what they are looking for when someone is thinking about suicide. But even if someone is not thinking about suicide, even if the person is depressed, they still need help. They need hope.

Be sure to have or be able to find some resources for someone who needs help. Even if you do not have them in hand, at least have an idea where to look on the Internet or in your local community. Several web sites listed in the back offer information on support groups in communities, and other web sites have information on books and other resources. Keep in mind the needs of the individual you are trying to help, and that will be your guide to the resources that can best help them. The bereaved person also might have been frustrated by the lack of resources or may not be thinking clearly and having a difficult time finding the needed information. Therefore, your help will be even more appreciated.

Be sensitive to the cultural and religious backgrounds of the people you are trying to help. They might be family and you might be familiar with their backgrounds but those backgrounds also can be different from your own. And if you are working with people whose background is not familiar to you, take the time to understand their background. That will help you comprehend their views on suicide and death and make it easier for you to help them. The goal is not to change how or what a person believes but to help them process their views and find comfort in the loss of someone they cared about.

Beliefs are not the only difference that can make working with other cultural groups a challenge. Actions can vary as much as beliefs. For instance, it might be acceptable for a person from another culture to take long pauses while speaking. The silence might be important to them and part of the story as they are telling it. A helper could be ready to jump in and say something, whereas the bereaved person is not finished and might get frustrated with the helper. The helper should be patient and allow people to take their time when speaking. In other cultures, it might not be acceptable for people to hug (the opposite of cultures and regions where hugging is very normal and an encouraged part of loss).

Be aware that touching another person might not be accepted. Asking the person is the best way to find out about his or her beliefs because information from other sources might not always be reliable for that person's cultural group, especially if there are deviations (maybe the majority does not hug but this particular person does).

As someone who wants to help a bereaved person, you are to be commended for wanting to reach out and provide support. Many people are too afraid to do what you are doing. It does not take a lot to help someone; mostly what is important is to be there for them and ask what they need. They will tell you and be grateful for what you offer.

You have the honor of accompanying them on this journey. The rocky road is not always an easy one and sometimes we need some help with it. The bereaved person may not always ask for help or even realize they need it. But listening to the bereaved, whether to the words they speak or their body language and actions, will give you some idea of how to guide them.

One of the aspects of the grief process that this book has focused on is finding meaning in the loss of someone we love, particularly after suicide. Sometimes it is through discussing the loss with someone else that we are able to find that meaning, to understand it, to figure out how it fits in our worlds. But we need guidance with the puzzle pieces; we need to look for the people who want to guide us on that path and help us put the pieces together.

Listeners pick up on clues, ideas, and other significant ideas that the bereaved might not hear in their own words. Listeners connect problems the person might be having that they are not able to put together themselves. Maybe they cannot piece together events that are related to the loss, yet someone who is listening can help them do that. New listeners are a new audience for the story.

Most of all, anyone who travels the grief journey with someone they care about is offering part of themselves that they probably did not realize they had to help the bereaved through what could be the most difficult experience in anyone's life.

- **Afterword** -

At the time of this writing, the idea of "posttraumatic growth" is emerging around the world. This concept says that people who have struggled with something very challenging in their lives can overcome it and emerge with positive transformation. Positive changes include increased appreciation for life (especially the people and routine things that we often take for granted), more meaningful relationships with others, changed priorities, increased personal strength, and a sense of a more connected spiritual life (Tedeschi & Calhoun, 2004). The authors of this study noted that for the people who experienced traumatic growth, it is not the trauma itself that caused the positive change but what happened to them after the trauma. And it was not a conscious goal; they simply were trying to survive.

Suicide is a trauma. It causes people to completely rethink everything about their lives. My family was no different than any other after Denise died. We had choices in how we reacted to Denise's suicide. While my parents had allowed Denise's previous suicide attempt to be hushed, because that is what Denise requested, after she died Mom was clear that there was no reason to keep it a secret. I can still hear her saying, "Maybe we can help someone else with her story."

Still, in the midst of grief, my intention was only to survive and understand why my sister had ended her life. How could I help others when I was confused about who I was because my sister had ended her life?

Often after my workshops on family suicide grief, I am asked how my family has coped with Denise's death and how the Linns are doing today.

Afterword

I am happy to report that the Linn family is doing pretty well. I mentioned in The Road Map chapter how Lois Bloom said that her son Sammy had made a choice and, thus, she and her husband Sam had choices after Sammy died. I do not believe we made a conscious choice as Iris Bolton said she did after her son Mitch died. Iris said her therapist told her she had a choice. While she could blame whomever she wanted, she also could take the opportunity to build a base for a stronger bond with her family (Peluso, 2002). Iris chose to help strengthen her family. My family chose to use Denise's death as a springboard to make us better people, and to appreciate each other more.

That is not to say that it was easy but we trudged along our road and emerged on the other side as better people. I believe that Denise's suicide was meant to help us help others. Through her story, I have no idea how many people I have educated about suicide and the people left behind. The numbers do not matter to me. It is more important to me to keep telling her story, and the stories of all the people I have met along my road; and help people, whether they are bereaved, want to help the bereaved, or just want to learn about the devastation that suicide can bring.

We have continued to keep Denise as a member of our family. We talk about her, and we try to help the two Linn grandchildren, Jordan and Britt, know who their aunt was. I realize that it is not the same in many families because most do not have an author and speaker who publicly tells the family's story. Still everyone has the same opportunity to include the deceased loved ones.

Just as no road or journey is static, the family system is constantly evolving, changing, and communicating. For families and the individuals who make up those families, the stories will change as the road is traveled. They are good markers of the journey. And as those stories change, they become part of each family's history, development, strength, and meaning.

When we venture on the healing journey, the road is all uphill. How we choose to continue from there is our choice. Getting started is the hard-

est part. We fear what we do not know. Yet by taking this journey, we find out that we are stronger than we ever thought. And we realize that our loved ones remain part of our lives in ways we never could have imagined. It is well worth the rocky road.

Let me help you start your journey before I end this book. I learned from someone else one way to end a support group is by allowing people to share a happy/funny memory of the loved one who has died. I used this in my own experience of running a group and I found it was a good way to tie up the hour or so of raw emotions and allow people to leave with hope as they ventured back into the world. As I close **Rocky Roads**, *I ask each one of you to think about a happy or funny story of your loved one. And may that story be the hope and inspiration that starts you on your healing journey.*

References

Berman, A. L. (in press).
Estimating the population of survivors of suicide: Seeking an evidence base. *Suicide and Life-Threeatening Behavior.*

Bloch, S. (1991).
A systems approach to loss. *Australian and New Zealand Journal of Psychiatry, 25,* 471–80.

Cain, A. C. (2002).
Children of suicide: The telling and the knowing. *Psychiatry, 65,* 124–36.

Cain, A. C. (2006).
Parent suicide: Pathways of effects into the third generation. *Psychiatry, 69*(3), 204–27.

Centers for Disease Control and Prevention, National Center for Injury Prevention and Control (2010).
Web-based Injury Statistics Query and Reporting System (WISQARS) [online]. WISQARS Fatal Injuries: Mortality Reports. (2010) [cited January 6, 2010]. Available from:*http://webappa.cdc.gov/sasweb/ncipc/mortrate.html.*

Cerel, J. (2010).
Those left behind: Research to better understand suicide survivors. Poster presentation at American Association of Suicidology Conference, Orlando.

The Compassionate Friends (2006).
When a child dies 2006 survey. Oakbrook, IL: The Compassionate Friends, downloaded from *http://tcf.fusion92.net/pdf/When_a_Child_Dies-2006_Final.pdf.*

Harwood, D., Hawton, K., Hope, T., & Jacoby, R. (2002).
The grief experiences and needs of bereaved relatives and friends of older people dying through suicide: A descriptive and case-control study. *Journal of Affective Disorders, 72,* 185–94.

Hedstrom, P., Liu, K.-Y., & Nordvik, M.K. (2009).
Interaction domains and suicide: A population-based panel study of suicides in Stockholm, 1991–1999. *Social Forces, 87*(2), 713–40.

Linn-Gust, M. (2001).
Do They Have Bad Days in Heaven? Surviving the Suicide loss of a Sibling. Albuquerque: Chellehead Works.

Linn-Gust, M. (2004).
Six survivors per suicide . . . who decided? *Surviving Suicide, 16*(3), 1, 7, 8.

Maple, M., Plummer, D., Edwards, H., & Minichiello, V. (2007).
The effects of preparedness of suicide following the death of a young adult child. *Suicide and Life-Threatening Behavior, 37*(2), 127–34.

Martin, T. L., & Doka, K.J. (2000).
Men don't cry...women do: Transcending gender stereotypes of grief. Philadelphia: Taylor & Francis.

McIntosh, J. L. (for the American Association of Suicidology) (2009).
U.S.A. suicide 2006: Official final data. Washington, DC: American Association of Suicidology, dated April 19, 2009, downloaded from http://www.suicidology.org.

Moos, N. L. (1995).
An integrative model of grief. *Death Studies, 19,* 337–64.

Peluso, P. R. (2002).
Counseling families affected by suicide: An interview with Iris Bolton. *The Family Journal: Counseling and Therapy for Couples and Families, 10*(3), 351–57.

Prigerson, H. G., Shear, M. K., Jacobs, S. C., Reynolds, C.F., III, Maciejewski, P. K., & Davidson, J. R., et al. (1999).
Consensus criteria for traumatic grief. A preliminary empirical test. *British Journal of Psychiatry, 174,* 67–73.

Qin, P., Agerbo, E., & Mortensen, P. B. (2002).
Suicide risk in relation to family history of completed suicide and psychiatric disorders: A nested case-control study based on longitudinal registers. *Lancet, 360*(9340), 1126–30.

Rando, T. A. (1993).
Treatment of complicated mourning. Champaign, IL: Research Press.

Runeson, B., & Asberg, M. (2003). Family history of suicide among suicide victims. *American Journal of Psychiatry, 160*(8), 1525–26.

Shneidman, E. (1972). Forward. In A. C. Cain (Ed.), *Survivors of Suicide*. Oxford: Charles C. Thomas.

Silverman, P. R., & Klass, D. (1988). Introduction: What's the problem? In D. Klass, P. R. Silverman, & S. L. Nickman (Eds.), *Continuing Bonds: New Understandings of Grief* (pp. 3–27). Philadelphia: Taylor & Francis.

Tedeschi, R. G., & Calhoun, L. G. (2004). Posttraumatic growth: Conceptual foundations and empirical evidence. *Psychological Inquiry, 15*(1), 1–18.

Walsh, F. (2003). Family resilience: A framework for clinical practice. Family Process, 42(1), 118.

Webster's New Universal Unabridged Dictionary (1996). New York: Barnes & Noble Books.

World Health Organization. (2010). Suicide Prevention: The Problem. Retrieved January 6, 2010, from http://www.who.int/mental_health/prevention/suicide/suicideprevent/en/.

Resources

Web Sites

The Internet has changed resources in ways we never could have imagined just a short time ago. The resources below are not comprehensive by any means. Instead, I have listed the major resources for the bereaved by suicide. The number of web sites has greatly increased over the years. It is easy to Google "bereaved by suicide or "suicide survivors" and get pages of links. I have included links below that I have found helpful and complete over the years. You also will find more links on all of these web sites. The first three listed offer comprehensive information for all facets of suicide (prevention, intervention, postvention). Further contact information is available on the sites.

American Association of Suicidology
www.suicidology.org

American Foundation for Suicide Prevention
www.afsp.org

International Association for Suicide Prevention
www.iasp.info

The Dougy Center for Grieving Children and Families
www.dougy.org

Suicide Prevention Action Network
www.spanusa.org

The Compassionate Friends Bereaved Parents and Siblings
www.thecompassionatefriends.org

Friends for Survival (national newsletter available)
www.friendsforsurvival.com

Suicide Information and Education Center
www.suicideinfo.ca

Suicide Prevention Resource Center
www.sprc.org

Internet Bereaved by Suicide Support Groups

The main web site is *www.pos-ffos.com*

To join POS (Parents of Suicides) or FFOS (Friends and Families of Suicides), the quickest way is to either email Karyl Chastain Beal (arlynsmom@bellsouth.net) and ask for an application, or to go to *http://health.groups.yahoo.com/group/parentsofsuicides/* to sign up for POS or to http://health.groups.yahoo.com/group/ffofsuicides/ to sign up for FFOS.

Other web sites:

www.siblingsurvivors.com
A web site specifically for siblings grieving a suicide loss; includes a public message board where siblings help each other grieve.

www.bereavedbysuicide.com
An international resource for the bereaved by suicide with articles and resources worldwide.

www.facesofsuicide.com
Faces of Suicide

www.suicidegrief.com
Suicide Grief Support Forum (public message board)

www.heartbeatsurvivorsaftersuicide.org

If you are worried about yourself or someone you care about in the United States, please call the National Suicide Prevention Lifeline at 1-800-273-TALK (www.suicidepreventionlifelife.org). You also can call this number if you are grieving and need support.

If you are in another country and seeking resources, the International Association for Suicide Prevention (www.iasp.info) web site offers information for various countries.

Books

This is a select list of books that I recommend to people when I'm asked. For more comprehensive lists, visit the American Association of Suicidology or American Foundation for Suicide Prevention web sites for indexes of books that have been approved for reading. As of the publication of this book, all the books listed below were available for sale via the Internet.

For Adults

After Suicide: Help for the Bereaved by Sheila Clark (Hill of Content, 1995). An easy-to-read book discussing the basics of suicide grief.

Do They Have Bad Days in Heaven? Surviving the Suicide Loss of a Sibling by Michelle Linn- Gust (Bolton Press 2001/Chellehead Works, 2002). The first comprehensive resource for sibling survivors of suicide and the precursor to *Rocky Roads*.

Healing After the Suicide of a Loved One by Ann Smolin and John Guinan (Fireside, 1993). A book I found very helpful in my most intense time of suicide loss.

A Long-Shadowed Grief: Suicide and its Aftermath by Harold Ivan Smith (Cowley, 2006). Harold Ivan Smith does a wonderful job discussing many perspectives of loss and offering prayers at the end of each chapter for those who find them comforting.

Leaving You: The Cultural Meaning of Suicide by Lisa Lieberman (Ivan R. Dee, 2003). Provides a historical perspective on suicide that helps to explain the stigma and shame suicide still endures today.

Mourning after Suicide: Looking Up by Lois Bloom (Pilgrim Press, revised 2004). A small booklet by Lois Bloom, whose son died by suicide. Easy reading for the bereaved who have difficulty focusing for long periods of time.

No Time to Say Goodbye: Surviving the Suicide of a Loved One by Carla Fine (Doubleday, 1997). Carla Fine's husband killed himself but this book gives many perspectives on the different relationships people have in their lives.

November of the Soul: The Enigma of Suicide by George Howe Colt (Scribner, 2006). This is the updated version of Colt's 1991 *The Enigma of Suicide*. Colt provides a comprehensive look at suicide including a historical perspective.

Touched by Suicide: Hope and Healing After Loss by Michael F. Myers and Carla Fine (Gotham, 2006). A psychiatrist (Myers) and a writer/survivor of suicide loss (Fine) come together in this book to offer hope in grieving a suicide loss.

Understanding Your Suicide Grief: Ten Essential Touchstones for Finding Hope and Healing your Heart by Alan Wolfelt (Companion Press, 2009). (Companion journal is listed below under the same name.)

Why People Die by Suicide by Thomas Joiner (Harvard University Press, 2005). Joiner, a survivor and researcher, helps untangle the mystery of why people take their lives.

For Children:

But I Didn't Say Goodbye: Helping Children and Families After a Suicide by Barbara Rubel (Griefwork Center, revised 2009). Barbara Rubel's book offers a story of a family, through the eyes of the son, after the father's suicide. Questions are presented at the end of the chapters for discussion.

Children Also Grieve: Talking about Death and Healing by Linda Goldman (Jessica Kingsley, 2006). A children's book with questions and places where children remember a loved one and learn about how to cope with loss.

The Invisible String by Patricia Karst (DeVorss, 2000). A simple children's story about how we're never alone even when separated from someone we love.

Someone I Love Died by Suicide: A Story for Child Survivors and those Who Care for Them by Doreen Cammarata (Grief Guidance, revised 2009).

For Teens:

After by Francis Chalifour (Tundra Books, 2005). A fictional account of a teen boy whose father dies by suicide.

God and I Broke Up by Katarina Mazetti (Groundwood Books, 2005). A fictional account of a teen girl whose friend dies by suicide.

Journals

For adults:

I Remember...I Remember by Enid Samuel Traisman (Centering, revised 2008).

The Understanding your Suicide Grief Journal: Exploring the Ten Essential Touchstones by Alan D. Wolfelt (Companion Press, 2009). (This book is a companion to the book above of the same name.)

For teens:

Fire in My Heart, Ice in My Veins: A Journal for Teenagers Experiencing a Loss by Enid Samuel-Traisman (Centering, revised 2009).

Healing Your Grieving Heart Journal for Teens by Alan Wolfelt and Megan Wolfelt (Companion Press, 2002).

For clinicians who work with the suicide bereaved:

Grief After Suicide: Understanding the Consequences and Caring for the Survivors by Jack Jordan and John McIntosh (Routledge, August 2010). The first book in almost twenty years to address the clinical issues around working with the suicide bereaved.

DVDs

THAW: Christmas at the Cemetery and *Grief: A Family Healing* (one DVD includes both short films) (Jeff Orgill)
Contact: Jeffreyjayorgill@gmail.com

After a Suicide (Diane Conn)
Contact: conndiane@aol.com

Music

"Miss you More than Words Can Say" by Mickey Coleman is available for listening at www.myspace.com/mickeycoleman1 and for purchase on his CD *Mother Lullaby* at www.mickeycoleman.com.

Before Their Time is a three-CD collection of songs and music written in memory of people who died young. Featuring original performances by the singer-songwriters and composers, this benefit album was produced by Michael Whitman, father of a young man who took his life. A music resource for people mourning the death of someone close, the music on *Before Their Time* brings comfort, healing, and hope, wrapped in a wide variety of musical styles, ranging from classics by internationally known artists to a few début songs and performances. All sales of the CDs benefit suicide prevention and hospice organizations. www.beforetheirtime.org.

- About the Author -

Michelle Linn-Gust, Ph.D., is an international author and speaker about suicide prevention and postvention issues as well as the importance of dog companionship, particularly after loss. She is the author of *Ginger's Gift: Hope and Healing Through Dog Companionship*. Her first book, based on the suicide of her younger sister Denise, *Do They Have Bad Days in Heaven? Surviving the Suicide Loss of a Sibling,* inspired siblings around the world in their survival after a loved one's suicide. She is the President-Elect for the American Association of Suicidology. Read more about Michelle at www.michellelinngust.com.